Dedicated to the memory of all 194 lives lost,
to their families and friends,
to all of those hundreds who became ill
and to the residents whose lives and livelihoods were impacted.

Front cover pictures

Top left (AR): Broadwater Reading Room operated as a Temporary Hospital, with two wards on the ground floor, for exactly two months from July 20th 1893. The gentleman on the left is leaning on one of the ninety temporary water tanks that had been placed around Worthing, Broadwater and West Tarring and three Nurses stand at the doorway.

Top middle (WSP): Ernest Tupper was a chimney sweep living in Newland Road. His six-year-old son, Harry, died from typhoid on August 26th 1893. In the October, Ernest wrote to the Sussex Coast Mercury to thank the nurses for the care of his six children who had become ill with typhoid.

Top right (WSP): The Travellers' Rest was a lodging house in Clifton Road before it was requisitioned as a Temporary Hospital from July 17th to early October 1893. It had capacity for eighty patients across eight wards on two floors. It was staffed by the Doctors and Nurses pictured here.

Main picture (WSP): Nurserymen gathered in Ham Road prior to their annual outing to Wisborough Green in 1892. The outing organiser, Abraham Duffield, is the gentleman on the left holding a cornet and standing behind three of his sons. He succumbed to enteric fever in Worthing Infirmary on May 27th 1893.

Back cover pictures

Top left (WL): Dr Charles Kelly was medical officer of health for West Sussex from 1874 till his death in 1904. He played a key role in the town's response to the 1893 typhoid epidemic.

Top middle (ML): Frederick Caesar and Kate Linfield with their two eldest children in a studio photograph. Frederick was a town councillor who - motivated by a strong faith and commitment to Christian values – became very involved in carrying typhoid victims from their homes to ambulances and the dead from the hospitals.

Top right (IR): Edward Cunningham Patching was Mayor of Worthing from 1891 to 1893.

Bottom (web): An image of the typhoid bacillus – just five microns in length.

FEVER!

The Year Worthing Died

A comprehensive account of the 1893 Worthing Typhoid Epidemic

Published by
Wiston Enterprises

Edited by Colin Reid
Contact email: halfscottish1@zen.co.uk

First published October 2023
© 2023 Friends of Broadwater & Worthing Cemetery.

Significant contributions by Chris Hare, Malcolm Linfield, Mary Mckeown,
Caroline Nelson, Colin Reid and Marion Woolgar.

Designed and produced by
Panda Creative Ltd, Sompting, West Sussex
www.pandacreativeltd.co.uk

Contents

Biographies of Contributors

Each contributor to this volume was invited to imagine they could step back in time and have a conversation with one person connected with the 1893 epidemic – these are appended to their personal biographies below:

Chris Hare was born in Worthing in 1962. He has been lecturing on and writing about Sussex history since 1987. He has written several books on local history topics and, for nine years, ran county history courses through the Centre for Continuing Education at the University of Sussex. For five years he was an adult education manager, both in Devon and in West Sussex.

He is currently director of History People UK Limited and manages several NLHF (National Lottery Heritage Fund) projects in the county. Recent projects include South Downs Generations (www.southdownsgenerations.org.uk), Worthing Village Voices (www.worthingvillagevoices.org.uk), and Belloc, Broadwood and Beyond (www.belloc-broadwood.org.uk).

Chris has a BA(Hons) in British Studies from the University of Brighton and an MA in Life History from the University of Sussex. He is a fully qualified adult education teacher. Since 1999, Chris has conducted over 100 oral history interviews with people living across the county, recording the details of their lives and the great changes they witnessed. Those interviewed were aged between 60 and 104 at the time of being interviewed. He has written many books on local and county history. His most recent book, *Hilaire Belloc, The Politics of Living,* was published in December 2022.

Conversation: If Chris could speak with William Churcher (one-time editor of the *Worthing Gazette*), he would ask: Was there a cover up, did he know anything about the 'obscene postcard' sent to Henshall Fereday, how did he cope with a braying mob outside his house and the death of his daughter? Lastly, did he know anything about the property of deceased residents passing to 'the forty thieves', and did this group even really exist?

Malcolm Linfield has always been fascinated by the past and has a particular interest in local and family history. He is chairman of a one-name family history society and enjoys writing articles for various publications and websites. For several years, he has been researching the Worthing Glasshouse Industry - a very much neglected part of Worthing's history and is currently writing a book on the subject which he hopes will go some way to remedy this unfortunate omission. Malcolm works as horticulture manager at a local charity for adults with learning disabilities and has been involved in social care for nearly 30 years.

Conversation: Malcolm would love to speak with his great grandfather: Arthur George Linfield senior.

Mary Mckeown is a founder member of The Friends of Broadwater and Worthing Cemetery. She became very interested in researching the typhoid victims after hearing about the epidemic very soon after joining that group. She thought it was so sad that the majority of victims had not been identified and felt that they should all be remembered. She has had an interest in genealogy and local history for many years and has been involved in WW1 and WW2 local history projects. Mary is also an active member of the H.M.S. Hood Association, and has helped to find photographs of the men lost for the association's memorial roll of honour.

Conversation: Every time Mary has found herself near the grave of Edith Hawksworth, she has been moved by the thought that there lies a nurse who died because of her decision to come to Worthing to look after typhoid victims. If only she could chat with her.

Caroline Nelson has worked for the NHS for over twenty years specialising in clinical audits and data quality. During the last five years, she has been studying part-time for a history degree. When one of the modules required her to analyse data for a local studies project, the little-known Worthing typhoid epidemic in 1893 seemed a logical choice. Caroline is a member of the Society of Genealogists and is researching her family history.

Conversation: If it were possible, Caroline would like to catch up with Margaret Mears – a 19-year-old housekeeper for her widowed father. On July 26th 1893, she died as a result of typhoid and a miscarriage.

Colin Reid was born in central Worthing in 1949 and, after attending Heene Primary School and Worthing High School for Boys, he studied electrical engineering at Bristol University. For a couple of years, he worked as a research engineer for Decca Radar but, he had a change of direction. The remaining 40 years of his employment was in the field of social work. In 2020, he published *My Dear Clarice* – a detailed history of his maternal ancestors. With a long-term interest in local history, he has been pleased to be involved in recording this account of the typhoid epidemic.

Conversation: Colin would welcome a chance to speak with the Rev Joseph Lancaster – a man of integrity and compassion and a victim of the typhoid epidemic.

Marion Woolgar is a family historian who has been researching her husband's family for the past 30 years. In 2010, she became interested in the Worthing typhoid epidemic of 1893 and strongly believes that the victims should be identified and recorded. Since then, Marion has worked with the Friends of Broadwater & Worthing Cemetery to try and locate all the relevant documents regarding the victims. Marion is a member of Sussex Family History Group, the Guild of One-Name Studies and the West Sussex Archives Society and enjoys her continuing research projects as and when her health permits.

Conversation: Marion's choice would be to speak with Robert Grevett – registrar for the district of East Preston for his reminiscences about the effects of the epidemic. His name or that of his deputy appears on the majority of the typhoid death certificates.

Foreword

I have been a member of the Friends of Broadwater & Worthing Cemetery since it was formed in 2008, first as their Research Co-ordinator and, from 2012, as Chairperson. During the summer months, we run themed tours of the cemetery based on the lives of those buried within its walls. I have watched with interest as information about the 1893 typhoid epidemic has been unearthed, from the initial stories included in our first typhoid tour to the completion of the mammoth task to definitively identify all the victims.

I witnessed first-hand, the time and effort put into bringing this all together into one volume; the dedication to the task and sheer determination to succeed (not to mention the personal cost involved in buying certificates) of Mary, Colin, Marion and Caroline. Adding to their research that of Malcolm Linfield and local historian Chris Hare, has resulted in a comprehensive record of the events that took place told from many different perspectives.

Colin's introduction not only paints a picture of life at the time of the epidemic but also prepares us for what we can expect to discover over the course of the following chapters. He merged the data together to create a cohesive whole. There is something in this book for everyone: the local politics at play; the lives affected; the selfless acts as people pulled together; the statistics.

You can dip in and out of the various chapters depending on your own personal interests in the subject. Chris Hare's chapter gives an in-depth account of local life at the time. He provides an insight into the actions of local councillors, the costly mistakes made and the desperate attempts to maintain Worthing's reputation as a seaside resort. Malcolm Linfield brings a much more personal view of things with stories of his relatives, their recollections and involvement as the consequences of the epidemic played out. The subject that inspired Marion's involvement in this project can be found in 'Relief Funds'. Her fascination with the content of the cash book from Thomas Evans' relief fund (found while working on another project) was just the beginning and it prompted her to spend many more hours researching the subject. If numbers are your passion, then you will love Caroline's 'Statistics' chapter. It has detailed information about which areas of the town had the most victims and even includes a map showing that distribution. Personally, I love the 'Snippets' chapter put together by Mary: little bites of information that place you right there at the time.

It was so important to everyone involved in this project that a book should be produced to collate the research carried out over many years and preserve it for future generations. Now that has been achieved and you have the chance to 'read all about it'. Oh, and don't forget to check out that definitive list of victims; maybe one of your ancestors is on it.

Debra Hillman
March 11th 2023

Preface

'Little did we think when we started this (Church) Magazine, what sad events we should have to chronicle before the first year of its existence was over... It is probable that for many years to come, 1893 will be remembered as the year of the great outbreak of typhoid fever in our neighbourhood.'

Rev (William) Douglas Springett DD, Rector of West Tarring from 1892 to 1898.

These combined observations for September and August 1893 by the rector of West Tarring in the church magazine are as good as any contemporaneous accounts of the impact of typhoid fever not just in West Tarring but also in the neighbouring village of Broadwater and the newly incorporated borough of Worthing. In modern times, local historians such as Paul Holden and Chris Hare have been factually correct with their opening comments to this episode in the history of Worthing and environs: 'The biggest civil disaster in Worthing's history was undoubtedly the typhoid epidemic of 1893.'[1] 'There was no year in the history of Worthing more traumatic than 1893 and no year that led to more bitterness or recrimination.'[2]

Observers of world history will be familiar with the depredations of the fourteenth century Black Death/ Plague, or the so-called Spanish Flu pandemic of 1918 and, of course, the Covid-19 pandemic is still impacting the lives of millions across the globe. However, what Dr Charles Kelly described as: *The Epidemic of Enteric Fever in 1893 in the Borough of Worthing (and) in Broadwater & West Tarring*[3] was of a different order. As we will see, this epidemic was wholly avoidable. Locally and nationally during the nineteenth century, there would be a small number of people who fell victim to typhoid fever and, occasionally, there would be mini-outbreaks but few that touch the severity and persistence of the epidemic that is the subject of this book.

One of our number (Caroline Nelson) recently coined the phrase: the *Typhoid Research Project* as a way of describing the combined efforts of Mary Mckeown, Caroline Nelson, Colin Reid and Marion Woolgar in diligently researching at personal cost to identify 194 deaths from the 1893 epidemic and we are so pleased to be joined by Chris Hare and Malcolm Linfield in producing what is, so far, the most comprehensive account available.

It is our hope that – as you read this book – you will be able to compare and contrast with your experience of Covid-19 how the crisis of 1893 was dealt with. What was the response of those in office and in authority, how did medical professionals react, what was the impact on individuals, families and businesses, was there emergency provision and was it effective, did some act 'above and beyond the call of duty' and what provision was made for those in financial need?

Colin Edward Reid
October 6th 2022

[1]*Holden, Paul. 'Typhoid, Bombs and Matron – the History of Worthing Hospital'. 1992*
[2]*Hare, Chris. 'Worthing, A History'. 2008*
[3]*Kelly, Charles MD, FRCP. 'The Epidemic of Enteric Fever in 1893 in the Borough of Worthing (and) in Broadwater & West Tarring'. 1894*

Acknowledgements

As editor, Colin Reid is pleased to acknowledge the following assistance:

Research Consultant: *Mary Mckeown.*

Research & writing: *Chris Hare, Malcolm Linfield, Mary Mckeown, Caroline Nelson, Colin Reid and Marion Woolgar. Research Assistance: Worthing Library, Worthing Museum, West Sussex Record Office, Martin Hayes, Paul Robards and Chris Green.*

Photographs: *(AR) Regis family collection, (BCA) Broughton Community Archive, (CH) Chris Hare, (CR) Colin Reid, (DH) Debra Hillman, (GH) Gill Heasman, (IR) Ian Richardson collection, (JH) Jeff Hillman, (JV) John Vaughan, (KM) Kois Miah, (ML) Linfield family collection, (MM) Mary Mckeown, (MW) Marion Woolgar, (QM) Quentin Macaque, (SR) Sally Roberts, (WL) Worthing Library, (WMA) Worthing Museum & Art Gallery, (WSP) West Sussex County Council Library Service.*

Proofreading: *Anita Hobbs, John Vaughan and Nikki Sheeran.*

Reviews: *Benjamin Leney and Paul Holden.*

Foreword: *Debra Hillman.*

Project Finance: *Sally Roberts and Debra Hillman.*

Index: *Lela Tredwell.*

List of Subscribers and Donors

Thanks are due to all those who paid for copies of the book before publication. Where an asterisk is applied to a name that identifies individuals who made additional donations. Their support and interest has helped make this book possible. Especial thanks is due to FBWC for the donation of £1,500 and to one anonymous donor who made available a substantial bridging loan.

Barbara Ayres*	Janice Jones	Sally Pratten
Peter Bandy	Joss Lambourne	Lynn Purkiss
Cathy Beaumont	Mike Lawton	Pauline Reed
Jon Collet	Benjamin Leney	Colin E Reid*
Fran Dingwall	Alan Lindfield	Ian Reid
Ian Entwistle	Harry Linfield	Carolyne Rich
Mrs Judy Excell	Malcolm Linfield	Paul Robards
Nicola Farley	Nick Linfield	Sally Roberts
Frank Ffitch*	Mary Mckeown*	Tracey Scott
Cathy Glynn-Davies	Stephen Myerscough	Dr Barbara Pilley Shaw
Alison Grace	Richard Nowak	Dawn Helen Stringer
Barbara & Kevin Hall	Tony & Linda Page	Charlotte Tittle
Gill Heasman	Humphrey & Lesley Palmer*	John Turley
Pauline Hickling	Rosemary Pearson	Nicholas Johnson Weller
Debra Hillman	Sheila & David Pople	Lucy Wessels
Paul Holden*	Tom Pople	Rosemary Westlake
Frances Jackson	Anne Powell	Tom Wye

Introduction

by Colin Reid

In the Preface to this book, mention was made of the four people who comprised the Typhoid Research Project. Here, it is helpful to explain how this project grew organically from the different perspectives of those individuals: As Marion Woolgar describes, in 2010, she was researching non-conformist records in the Worthing area when she stumbled on a cash book entitled 'Epidemic Relief Fund 1893/94'[1] – she was captivated by the contents and a long-term interest in the epidemic began. Marion quickly became aware that the majority of the typhoid victims had been laid to rest in the Broadwater & Worthing Cemetery in South Farm Road and she made contact with the 'Friends' of that cemetery (FBWC). Marion was given a lot of help from various members of FBWC.

From the inception of FBWC in 2008 under the chairmanship of Major Tom Wye, there had been recognition that a large number of typhoid victims were buried in the cemetery and, among others, Mary Mckeown, who identified with the trauma for individuals and families, assisted in early research. In July 2011, 'The Typhoid Epidemic' was taken as the subject for a FBWC guided tour of the cemetery and a booklet was produced that included short biographies of 24 victims buried there. In that autumn, Marion published her article: 'Afflicted Worthing'[2] under the auspices of the West Sussex Archives Society. Then, as 2013 approached (the 120th anniversary of this catastrophe), Mary Mckeown made the case for a second, anniversary tour of the cemetery and for the installation of a long-overdue marble memorial at the entrance to the cemetery. The accompanying tour booklet included 16 more biographies and a list of 120 victims that had been identified from death certificates. Colin Reid was one of the researchers involved that year and, with his long interest in the history of his hometown of Worthing, he became keen to add to the public's knowledge and understanding of the events in 1893.

In 2010, Marion Woolgar – as a bona fide researcher – applied to the Registrar General for special permission to see the death registers for East Preston district for the period April to December 1893, but that request was unequivocally refused. The two 1894 official reports on the epidemic by Doctors Kelly[3] and Thomson[4] included no names of individual victims, nor were they contained in council records. The researchers confirmed the identity of some victims by purchasing death certificates for the small number of names mentioned in newspapers, magazines, school log books etc and by using 'inspired guesswork' for other purchases – inevitably, many of the certificates purchased recorded non-typhoid causes of death.

By coincidence, an Open University student (Caroline Nelson) had chosen the epidemic as the subject for one of her assignments and had already purchased a number of death certificates before she had made contact with FBWC. The four members of the Typhoid Research Project were now able to conclude they were within a 'gnat's whisker' of identifying all of the 1893 victims and, by August 2021, further purchases of certificates resulted in the identification of 194 deaths attributable to typhoid.

With encouragement from the present chairman of FBWC (Debra Hillman), plans were made to publish a comprehensive account of the epidemic by 2023 (the 130th anniversary). Meanwhile, in September 2022, a third tour of the cemetery entitled 'The Typhoid Epidemic – a Final Tribute' was organised. Fifteen more biographies were included in the accompanying booklet; and the names, ages and occupations of all 194 victims were read aloud to the 126 visitors to this tour, which was recorded on a video camera. Additionally, Debra Hillman had worked hard to produce 164 markers for the graves of those buried in the cemetery and a drone was employed to capture an aerial view.

Over the years, many authors have referred to this epidemic in books, papers and magazines – they include Paul Holden[5] and Barrie Keech[6] but, without doubt, it's difficult to imagine a more compelling analysis than that provided by Chris Hare in his book: *Worthing, A History*[7]. Chris readily agreed to revise his account and it appears in this book as chapter 2: 'Fever Year and the "Forty Thieves". There, Chris makes passing reference to those who acted more honourably, including Councillor F C Linfield and his brother, Arthur George Linfield. A descendant of the latter, Malcolm Linfield, had already written about his forbears in 1995 and, in chapter 3 ('A Better Way'), he provides a much more detailed account under the banner: 'The Linfield Brothers'. Additionally, opportunity is taken to recognise others who – while going about their business – acted nobly but succumbed to this awful disease.

While we await for the conclusions of the public inquiry into the response to the Covid-19 pandemic by the United Kingdom Government, by local authorities, by the National Health Service, by the social care system etc, with the 1893 typhoid epidemic we have the advantage of two official reports that appeared less than a year after the end of the epidemic. We have also been able to garner a lot of information from local and national newspapers, church magazines, school log books and a small number of first-hand accounts. Consequently, it has been possible to produce a comprehensive account of the 'Care & Treatment of Victims' (chapter 4) and of the 'Relief Funds' (chapter 5) that sprang up.

The information provided from the individual death certificates and from burial records has been used to provide the reader with a 'Complete List of Typhoid Deaths' (chapter 6) and, in chapter 7, Caroline Nelson has done a sterling job bringing together the data mentioned above with an analysis that stands alongside opinion and speculation. Finally, in chapter 8, Mary Mckeown has spent hours diligently scouring different collections to bring together a large selection of 'Snippets' that add colour to this account of a most significant event in the history of Worthing.

As indicated above, a good number of biographies of victims have been produced: Marion Woolgar appended some 89 to her WSAS essay, a further 21 have been newly researched for the booklets that accompanied three 'Typhoid Tours' of Broadwater Cemetery – and in chapter 3 appears one new biography. Consideration was given to providing the reader with a complete set of 194 biographies, but that was rejected because of the extra work needed and the extra space required – that could be the basis for a complementary publication at some future date.

---

[1] West Sussex Record Office reference NC/M5W/2/1/6/1

[2] Woolgar, Marion. 'West Sussex Archives Society Journal – Volume 79'. 2011

[3] Kelly, Charles MD, FRCP. 'The Epidemic of Enteric Fever in 1893 in the Borough of Worthing (and) in the Villages of Broadwater & West Tarring'. 1894

[4] Thomson, Theodore, Dr. 'Report to the Local Government Board on an Epidemic of Enteric Fever in the Borough of Worthing and in the Villages of Broadwater and West Tarring'. 1894

[5] Holden, Paul. 'Typhoid, Bombs and Matron – the History of Worthing Hospital'. 1992

[6] Keech, Barrie. 'Doctors, Dentists and Death – West Sussex Health Issues since the 19th Century'. 2011

[7] Hare, Chris, Worthing, A History. 2008

Chapter 1
Setting the Scene

by Colin Reid

Given the subject of this book, this chapter provides the reader with three introductory overviews: A description of life in Worthing in the early 1890s; a description of typhoid fever; and a pen picture of one character who had a central role before, during, and after the epidemic.

WORTHING IN THE EARLY 1890s

Charter Year – 1890:

On June 6th 1888, the Incorporation Committee of the Worthing Local Board produced a report that recommended active steps should be taken toward incorporation with West Worthing (Heene parish); and it was noted the West Worthing Commissioners were in agreement with this. A great deal of joint work then ensued that led to Queen Victoria giving her official blessing to the conferring of borough status on an expanded Worthing on August 15th 1890.

In his book: *Worthing, A History,*[1] Chris Hare powerfully illustrates how 1890 was a year of scandal after scandal in Worthing. Plans then to properly celebrate 'Charter Day' on Wednesday September 3rd must have come as something of a relief. By coincidence, Wednesday was also the normal publishing day for the *Worthing Gazette*. On that day the first edition didn't become available till after 5pm, giving opportunity not only to cover the steps leading to incorporation but also to describe in great detail all of the celebrations that day. In his 1990 book: *Centenary – One Hundred Years of the Borough of Worthing,*[2] Rupert Taylor could add little to the content within the *Gazette* article.[3] In my opinion, the organising committee – operating to a tight time schedule – produced a magnificent programme of events through the day that gave space

▼ *Just one example of the efforts to make 'Charter Day' a memorable occasion for ordinary members of the public in Worthing (WSP).*

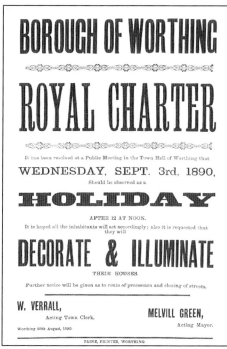

▲ On September 3rd 1890, huge crowds gathered to hear William Verrall (town clerk) read out extracts of the Charter from a specially constructed platform in front of the (Old) Town Hall (WSP).

▼ Worthing Town Council 1890/91. Left to right: Standing: Tupper, W Sams, Clark, Walter Butcher, Aldermen Robert Piper & C C Cook, William Verrall (town clerk), Alderman Edward Thomas Cooksey, George Purser, Augustine Birrell, Churcher and unknown. Seated on chairs: unknown, T Elliott, Alderman Edwin Lephard, Mayor Alfred Cortis, Alderman Edward Cunningham Patching, King, Kempster Knight & H Lea (Lee). Sitting on floor: Ewen Smith, F C Linfield, Alfred Crouch and William Walter (WSP).

for the acting town clerk (William Verrall) to proclaim extracts of the Charter from a specially constructed platform in front of the (Old) Town Hall.

As early as June 11th, there had been agreement that the borough of Worthing should be divided into five wards: East, Central, North-East, North-West and West. During October there was a great deal of canvassing votes for places on the new Town Council. This concluded with a municipal election on November 1st of 26 men, who used their first council meeting on November 10th to unanimously elect Alfred Cortis as the first mayor of the borough and to confirm the elevation of six of their number to that of aldermen. The latter necessitated the election of six more councillors on November 24th. It was not until 1902 before the neighbouring villages of Broadwater and West Tarring were absorbed into the borough of Worthing.

On November 9th 1891, at a meeting of the full council, Alderman Robert Piper proposed that Alderman Edward Patching should be elected mayor for the coming year. That was agreed unanimously and Alderman Piper was invited to take the role of deputymayor. Exactly a year later, Alderman Cortis proposed and it was unanimously agreed that Alderman Patching should continue as mayor for a further year, with Alderman Piper continuing as his deputy – so it was that Alderman Edward Cunningham Patching was mayor of Worthing for virtually the whole period of the typhoid epidemic. The full council for that crucial period comprised:

◀ *Alderman Edward Cunningham Patching, Mayor of Worthing 1891 to 1893 (IR).*

Mayor Patching, Deputy Mayor Piper, Aldermen A Cortis, C C Cook, E T Cooksey and E Lephard with Councillors G Baker, W J Butcher, H Chapman, W F Churcher, T Elliott, A B S Fraser, J Haywood, J H L Hine, K W Knight, H Lea, F C Linfield, T P Lund, G Purser, J Roberts, W Sams, G Ewen Smith, W Tupper, W Walter, W Verrall (town clerk) and C Baldwin (assistant clerk).

On June 28th 1893, the *Worthing Gazette* reported:

> 'The townspeople will generally regret to learn that his Worship the Mayor (Alderman Patching) has been very indisposed for some days past, owing doubtless to the considerable amount of mental anxiety occasioned by his domestic and official duties during the past few weeks. We are glad, however, to be able to state that Alderman Patching was sufficiently well to be able to leave Worthing for Tunbridge Wells this afternoon, and the burgesses will re-echo our wish that a few days' rest and change will effect a speedy restoration of his health.'

During July, Alderman Piper – as deputy mayor – stood in for Mayor Patching in his official duties.

The Town Council meeting of November 9th 1893 was not attended by the same concord. Despite entreaties by Alderman Cortis for unanimity to prevail for electing Alderman Robert Piper as mayor for 1893-94, Councillor Captain Fraser alleged that Alderman Piper had supported Mayor Patching in suppression of Dr Crookshank's report. Councillors Fraser, Goldsmith and Raffety voted against Alderman Piper assuming the role of mayor, while Councillors Collet and Fletcher abstained. Nevertheless, Alderman Robert Piper was elected as mayor.

A Contemporary View of Worthing:

Long's Worthing Directory for 1892[4] affords the following description of Worthing in 1891:

> 'WORTHING is situated on the coast of Sussex, about 10 miles west of Brighton, and 56 from London. Worthing, in the parish of Broadwater, and West Worthing, in the parish of Heene, are now incorporated, and deservedly rank as a fashionable watering place and health resort. The population is 16,606.
>
> The beautiful scenery of the neighbourhood, the charming walks and drives, the fine esplanade, and the holiday rambles which may be taken along the seashore, or on the lovely Downs, entitle it to rank as the former, while the remedial influence of its climate in disease, its good drainage, its pure and plentiful water supply, and its nearness to the Metropolis, place it foremost among the health resorts of the kingdom.
>
> The eminent Dr Tanner says: "Lying a few miles west of Brighton, and with an aspect almost due south, this town is fully exposed to the sun's rays. It is sheltered from the hot winds of summer, and the cold of winter, by the South Down hills, which have an average height of 600 feet. Hence it is warm in winter until the middle of February, and cool in summer; the air being neither too embracing nor too sedative. The mean temperature for the year is about 51°. The rainy days are fewer, and the quantity of rain that falls is less than at Ventnor or the west of England. During the summer the fine sands afford excellent bathing."'

The National Census, taken on the night of April 5th 1891, revealed Worthing had a population of 16,606 while that for Broadwater was 1,096 and West Tarring was 1,035. These combined totals represent a massive increase in population over the first nine decades of the century – little wonder then that, by 1891, there were eleven public schools in the area in addition to private schools. Likewise, there had been a proliferation of places of worship – no longer limited to St Mary's Broadwater, St Andrew's West Tarring and an Independent Chapel in Montague Street, there were now 23 churches of every possible persuasion.

All the necessary provision for a thriving community was in evidence: Two banks and a building society; three fire stations; a police station manned by 18 policemen; an infirmary; 16 doctors; three dentists; a gas works; swimming baths; a rugby club; a football club; cricket clubs; a cyclists' club; rowing and boating clubs; and clubs for chess and bird fanciers. Each August there was an offshore Rowing Regatta. There was no shortage of shopkeepers and businesses and, for the visitor, there was an abundance of lodging houses alongside hotel provision.

Given all of this, the members of Worthing Council and ordinary residents had every reason to face the years ahead with a good degree of optimism. As Chris Hare vividly describes in chapter 2, those hopes were to be dashed following an occurrence on April 14th 1893 that released a tiny bacterium into the town's water supply.

• • •

TYPHOID FEVER/ENTERIC FEVER

Much of the following is informed by the NHS website at www.nhs.uk/conditions/typhoid-fever/ . Typhoid fever is a bacterial infection that can spread throughout

the body, affecting many organs. Without prompt treatment, it can cause serious complications and can be fatal. It is caused by a bacterium called Salmonella Typhi. [Drs Kelly and Thomson in their 1894 reports were wont to call it *Bacillus typhosus* and *enteric fever Bacillus* respectively.] These bacteria live only in humans – not animals. If typhoid fever isn't treated up to one in five people with the condition will die.

Symptoms:
- A persistent high temperature that increases each day – as much as 104 degrees Fahrenheit.
- Headache
- Aches and pains.
- Fatigue.
- A cough.
- Constipation.
- Later sickness, stomach ache and diarrhoea.
- Distended abdomen.
- Possible rose-coloured skin rash, 'rose spots'.
- Then possible intestinal haemorrhaging or perforation.
- Bronchitis or pneumonia.

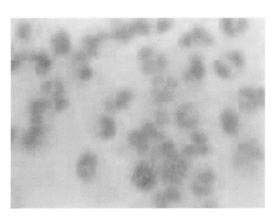

▲ *Typhoid rash
–'rose spots' –
typically may appear
on the lower chest/
upper abdomen. They
are 2 to 4 millimetres
in diameter.*

Transmission:
- Water or other fluids (eg milk) contaminated with faecal material.
- Poor hygiene of an infected person (faeces or (rarely) urine) before preparing food.
- Oral or anal sex with an infected person.

Treatment:
- Antibiotics.
- Oral rehydration if diarrhoea is a factor.
- Surgery for such as perforation of intestine.

• • •

CHARLES KELLY

In July 1904, the following glowing tribute was published in the *British Medical Journal*[5] and reproduced in the *Worthing Gazette*[6]:

> 'As a personal friend of the late Dr Charles Kelly, I should like to add my quotum as to the great loss which the medical profession especially in this town and neighbourhood have sustained by his death at a comparatively early age. He was one of the most original, clever and genial men I met. It was always a treat to me – nay even a privilege – to have 'a walk and talk' with him, which not infrequently happened; and I never parted from him after one of such conversations without feeling the better and the wiser. He was a real friend to all of us doctors in Worthing, and ever ready

to give his valuable opinion and advice (albeit in a most modest way) whenever it was asked of him. There was never the slightest friction between him and the members of the medical profession in this town which is, perhaps, the highest encomium which I can bring forward in his favour.'

(Mr W L'Heureux Blankarne of Vernon Lodge, Grafton Road)

Charles Kelly was born in Market Deeping, Lincolnshire on October 25th 1844. His parents were James Kelly (a surgeon from Athlone, Ireland) and Eliza Clifton who married on June 28th 1836 in Bourne, Lincolnshire. James and Eliza set up home in Market Place, Mill Lane, Market Deeping and all five of their children (Margaretta, Maria, James, Charles and Alfred) were born in that town between 1840 and 1846. By 1851, they were living in the same house where the children had a live-in governess with a teaching assistant; and Charles was still in the family home by 1861.

Soon afterward, Charles left to study at King's College London, winning, among other distinctions, a Warneford scholarship and the Leathes, Todd and Warneford prizes. He graduated as a Bachelor of Medicine and became a MRCS in 1866. The following year, he became a Doctor of Medicine and received the Gold Medal for that year. He had taken up a number of junior appointments at King's College Hospital where he was elected to the staff as assistant physician in 1869. He also took on that role at the Evelina Hospital for Sick Children. His lodgings were in Wimpole Street.

In 1874, he resigned his hospital posts on his appointment as medical officer of health for West Sussex. He briefly took up residence in Horsham, but was living in Broadwater Road, Worthing by the time of his marriage to Florence Hyde in Holy Trinity Church in her hometown of Hendford, Somerset on July 8th 1875. She was the ninth of ten children to Rev William Hyde, one time rector of Donyatt Parish Church in Somerset and Emma (nee Allen) who hailed from Crew in the city of Lincoln. Charles and Florence looked after their first two children (Arthur and Evelyn) at their home in Broadwater Road but, at least by 1891, they had moved to their long-term home at Ellesmere in Gratwicke Road with the addition of two more children (William and Florence).

▲ *Dr Charles Kelly – photographed in the studio of Walter Gardiner (WL).*

From 1875 right through to 1902, Dr Kelly published detailed and well-researched West Sussex health reports. In the early years, he took particular interest in 'ages at death' and in suicide as the cause of death, but every subject he covered resulted in voluminous reports attended by charts and statistics. In his book: *Doctors, Dentists and Death*[7], Barrie Keech not only takes a closer look at Dr Kelly's impressive research but also describes his active work across the county, his role as superintendent of the Isolation Hospital at Swandean and his ongoing commitment to King's College, where he was a Fellow, as Professor of Hygiene and Public Health.

Tragically, it is not for any of these labours that Dr Kelly will be remembered. Rather, it is for his role in what Paul Holden described as: 'The biggest civil disaster in Worthing's History – the Typhoid Epidemic of 1893'. This theme will be continued on in subsequent chapters.

Following the end of the epidemic, Dr Kelly produced a typically thorough report on June 30th 1894;[8] and his research and account informed the work of Dr Theodore Thomson whose report was completed on June 11th 1894.[9] Thereafter, Dr Kelly diligently continued in his post as medical officer for West Sussex. Indeed, he contributed to a meeting of the Worthing Town Council Sanitary Committee on the evening of June 14th 1904, appeared on good form and was looking forward to a long overdue holiday. The next day, feeling ill he took to bed and was attended by Dr Gostling. His condition worsened on the Thursday June 16th and he died in his Gratwicke Road home at 5pm from haematemesis – internal bleeding.

The *Worthing Gazette* reported[10] 'there was a considerable gathering' at Broadwater Cemetery on the following Monday such that a large number couldn't fit in the cemetery chapel for the funeral service conducted by the vicar of St Paul's Church, Rev E J Cunningham. That newspaper described 'The sudden death of Dr Kelly' as a 'Great loss to West Sussex' for 'His long period of Public Service'. Official obituaries appeared in the *British Medical Journal*[11] and The Lancet.

His widow, Florence, moved to 'Kilrush', Eton Road and remained a Worthing resident – albeit with visits to her daughter, Evelyn Barnes, in Devon. She died at home in the Eardley Hotel, Marine Parade on May 10th 1936 and she was laid to rest three days later in the same Broadwater Cemetery plot as her husband.

◀ *Front cover of Dr Kelly's report published June 30th 1894. (WL).*

REPORT ON THE EPIDEMIC
OF
ENTERIC FEVER
IN 1893.
IN THE
BOROUGH OF WORTHING.
IN
BROADWATER, AND IN WEST TARRING.
BY
CHARLES KELLY. M.D., F.R.C.P.
MEDICAL OFFICER OF HEALTH FOR WEST SUSSEX
PROFESSOR OF HYGIENE IN KINGS COLLEGE, LONDON

Brighton
THE SOUTHERN PUBLISHING CO., LTD., 130, NORTH STREET.
1894

[1] Hare, Chris. 'Worthing, A History'. 2008
[2] Taylor, Rupert. 'Centenary – One Hundred Years of the Borough of Worthing'. 1990
[3] Worthing Gazette for September 3rd 1890
[4] 'Long's Worthing Directory 1892'. 1892
[5] Blankarne, Mr W L'Heureux. British Medical Journal for July 9th 1904
[6] Worthing Gazette for July 14th 1904
[7] Ibid.
[8] Ibid.
[9] Ibid.
[10] Worthing Gazette for June 22nd 1904
[11] British Medical Journal for July 2nd 1904

Chapter 2

Fever Year and the 'Forty Thieves'

by Chris Hare

There was no year in the history of Worthing more traumatic than 1893 and no year that led to more bitterness or recrimination. For this was when the town was ravaged by typhoid fever. Not only did 194 people die and at least another 1,222 become seriously ill – sometimes being bedridden for weeks or even months – but there were also accusations of incompetence and the suppression of vital information by members of the Town Council, including the mayor. In the aftermath of 'the fever,' it was claimed that certain prominent townspeople enriched themselves, and so was born the local legend of the 'Forty Thieves'. This chapter seeks to untangle the facts from the fiction and to establish what really happened in those dark days of 1893.

Seaside resorts during the nineteenth century sold themselves, not so much on hours of sunshine or the 'congeniality of the climate', important as these things were, but on the resort's mortality figures. In short, the prospective visitor wished to be assured that he would be staying in a resort that would improve his health and increase, rather than detract from his life expectancy. Outbreaks of cholera, typhus and typhoid were not uncommon in nineteenth-century England and such outbreaks caused panic when they occurred. All three of these diseases were linked to the contamination of drinking water by sewage. Visitors were also, therefore, very keen to know that the resort had a good, fresh supply of water and that the removal of human waste was ensured by an effective sewerage system that was enclosed and separated from the water mains.

The establishment of the Worthing Town Commissioners in 1803 had included establishing appropriate sanitary provision in the town and, by 1814, it was stated that the raw sewage, that had run freely through the streams and ditches of the town, was now fully enclosed. However, Worthing depended on wells for drinking water and many properties disposed of their sewage in cesspools – not an ideal combination. However, no serious outbreak of disease occurred and in 1850, Worthing was proud to declare that 'there is only one town in the kingdom where fewer deaths occur, in proportion to the number of inhabitants.'[1] However, not everyone in Worthing was so sanguine, a body of opinion, that for simplicity's sake, we can refer to as 'the progressives,' believed that the town should do far more to improve its sanitary arrangements, as it was more by good fortune than design that the town had not experienced a public health epidemic. Against this point of view were others within the town, whom we can call 'the conservatives,' who saw innovation in this regard as an unnecessary and, more to the point, costly policy that would have to be borne by the ratepayers. It was more than drains and sewers that divided the progressives and the conservatives and led to various disputes, often of a violent nature within the town.[2]

In 1852, the progressives succeeded in replacing the Worthing Town Commissioners with the Worthing Local Board of Health (the 'Local Board') that would henceforth act as the town's local government and, as the name suggests, have enhanced powers to improve sanitary provision within the town, to be charged to the rates. After 1871, it was also possible to raise money for 'extraordinary improvements' from the Local Government Board. Between 1853 and 1857, the new Worthing Board did greatly improve the sewage, drainage and water supply in Worthing. Most notably, a water tower was built north of the High Street. Water was pumped by engines, from new boreholes, into a large holding tank, from where gravity would allow the water to be provided to the growing number of homes in the town.

Owen Breads, one of the young progressives, in his *New Guide and Hand-Book to Worthing* of 1859, hailed the improvements that had brought fresh water to each house in the town as well as providing an outfall of sewage 'to a distance' from the town. Previously, all Worthing's sewage had been deposited onto the sands and left for the sea to carry away at the next high tide. However, Breads also noted that the improvements had taken place in the face of 'considerable opposition.'[3] This resistance was manifest in the columns of Worthing's short-lived newspaper, *The Monthly Record*, which had described the £5,000 costs of the improvements as being

▼ *Waterworks and water tower 1857. After 1893, it was known as the 'Fever Tower', but it wasn't demolished until 1924 (WSP).*

◀ Nurserymen gathered in Ham Road prior to their annual outing to Wisborough Green in 1892. Several of these men died of typhoid fever during the 1893 epidemic, including the outing organizer, Abraham Duffield, standing fourth from right holding a cornet (WSP).

'excessive and out of all proportion to the probable requirements of the town.'[4] Owen Breads was involved in a scandalous altercation with his opponents in 1869 and was forced out of the town due to the level of animosity directed towards him.

In actual fact, the 'excessive' improvements were, within thirty years, showing themselves to be inadequate to the demands being made upon them. Between 1851 and 1891, the population of Worthing increased three-fold, rising to over 16,000 inhabitants. In 1882, it was being reported that during the summer months, the water tower tank was empty by midday.[5] In 1885 a third well was dug at the water tower site in order to meet the growing demand. The following year, Herbert Jordan was elected to the Local Board, having made the provision of a safe and reliable water supply the central focus of his appeal to the electorate. There had been a contained outbreak of typhoid in 1880 and Jordan realised that the sinking of yet more wells at a time when the number of cesspools was proliferating, was not a wise policy. He was an early advocate of pumping water from the Downs into *Worthing* – a costly, yet effective procedure, free from the risk of contamination. Although speaking the language of the progressives, Jordan had many friends amongst the conservatives. Even that arch die-hard, George French (editor of the Worthing *Gazette* and hugely influential in the town) declared that Worthing was 'indebted' to Jordan for persuading the Local Board to undertake an analysis of the town's existing drinking water.[6] By 1888, however, Jordan was becoming alarmed at the lack of progress and warned of the dangers that could result should the existing wells become contaminated. His bid to be elected as a county councillor in January 1889 was thwarted when he lost, by a few votes to Edward Patching.[7] Alas for Worthing, Jordan died, at a relatively young age, in 1890, a moment marked 'with unfeigned regret,'[8] by the *Worthing Intelligencer*, the newspaper most closely associated with the progressive point of view.

In March 1893 (by which time the town had been incorporated and the Board was replaced by a town council), further excavations were commenced at the waterworks site, with a view to locating a new supply of water. On the afternoon of Friday April 14th, the resident engineer, R J Harris, was called away from his lunch, as workers reported a surge of water, rising in one of the shafts. At first, Harris thought it was sea water, but on tasting it he found it to be fresh. Men were employed to secure the shaft, working shifts to line it with bricks. Despite evidence, that later came forward, that there was often 'a bad smell' from the new well in the mornings, local councillors and the local press, were delighted that Worthing's water problems were now over, thanks to the discovery of the 'Big Fissure.'[9]

Yet within a few weeks there were reports of severe diarrhoea in the town, and then, on May 8th, two people were seen by a town doctor, suffering from a high fever. Within a week there were 60 cases, and within a month, 38 people had died. On May 23rd, Dr Charles Kelly, West Sussex Medical Officer of Health (resident in Worthing), formally informed the Local Government Board that there was an outbreak of typhoid fever in Worthing. Initially, the town, at least its better placed section, appeared united in its efforts to play down the significance of the outbreak for fear of destroying the holiday season, on which the economy of the resort depended. None of the local newspapers ran any stories on the outbreak, although all must have been all too aware of the danger they were facing. A decision was taken to 'flush out' the system. It is not recorded how this was done, but possibly sea water was pumped into the mains, hydrants and dead-ends. The tank on the water tower was also cleansed. The Town Sanitary Committee was convinced that this effort had solved the problem, and indeed following these measures, new cases of fever declined markedly, until on June 14th, Dr Kelly, with the full support of the mayor and Sanitary Committee, declared that 'the epidemic may now be considered at an end.'[10] The Mayor, Edward Patching, no stranger to controversy, was in bullish mood and resolved to ride out the storm. In a joint statement with William Verrall, the town clerk, and Charles Cook, chairman of the Sanitary Committee, he issued an 'Official Communication to the London Press', which put the blame for the outbreak on the nocturnal habits of the brick-setters, employed in lining the new well, back in April.[11]

Mayor Patching and the Sanitary Committee were playing a dangerous game. They were gambling on the measures they had already taken being sufficient to stem the epidemic and thereby ensure that the summer season at Worthing would not be undermined by the spectre of disease. However, the measures they had taken had not been sufficient, as the cause they attributed to the outbreak – the nocturnal habits of the night workers – had not been the cause of the epidemic, but rather contamination from an old sewer, close to the new well. Far more seriously, it would later be alleged that Mayor Patching knew this was the case but had suppressed this vital information. However, the councillors were delighted as the visitors kept coming to Worthing during June. During the second week of the month, 250

▼ Looking east along Marine Parade during the hot summer of 1893 – possibly days before the surge in typhoid infection (WSP).

members of the Borough Hop Trade Mutual and Friendly Society spent the day in the town[12] and Patching claimed that there had been 10,000 visitors during June.

However, this was only a lull as the terrible epidemic came back with a vengeance at the beginning of July, with devastating consequences. There is little doubt that this was not a second outbreak, as reported in the press, but a reoccurrence of the original outbreak. The bacteria may have been in abeyance due to the 'flushing-out' of the system, but its source and cause – faecal contamination – was still present. There also seems little doubt that the weather – dry and hot – caused the bacteria to proliferate. *The West Sussex Gazette* reported on June 22nd: 'No rain! No rain! Things are beginning to look serious as regards the weather. Since the first week of March, there has been hardly enough wet to lay the dust.'[13] When the rains did come, and then only for a few weeks until the hot and dry conditions returned, they may have simply washed more of the bacteria into the drinking water supply. Whatever the exact process that led to the resurgence of 'the fever,' the toll on the town's population was immediate and terrible. In the first week of July, 184 cases were reported, rising to 819 cases by the middle of the month, with 65 deaths.[14] As the month progressed, so the epidemic spread, first to Broadwater, then to Tarring and finally, on July 27th, to West Worthing. Many of the cases in these outlying areas were caused not by victims drinking contaminated water, but by close association with those already infected. With an incubation period of up to two weeks, the opportunities for spreading the disease were considerable and would eventually lead to over 1,416 cases being reported, of whom 194 were to die.

No longer could the Worthing press ignore the situation, hoping all would be well, indeed the old partisanship between progressives and conservatives resurfaced, with real rancour being displayed on the editorial pages. While the *Worthing Gazette* sought

▲ *On July 7th 1893, Richmond House was the first building to be converted for use as a temporary hospital. The doctors, nurses and supporters have been identified: Four men at the back: Drs Hinds, Dickson, Parker & Opie. Women standing: Caroline, Marjorie, Godfrey, Hoare, Miss Bothamly, Ford, Passant, Ketley & Maiben. Sitting: Mr A Collet, Baines, Mrs Horton (matron, holding dog), Johnson & Mr Simpson (WSP).*

to champion the council, one of whose members, William Churcher was both its proprietor and editor (French having died in 1887); the *Worthing Intelligencer* began to carry increasingly shrill criticism of the council. In particular, it published letters from Dr John Goldsmith, a former member of the old Local Board, who claimed that the mayor had suppressed a report by Professor Crookshank of King's College, London, which showed that the water from the High Street works was still being contaminated.[15] Patching claimed that he had only acted in the best interests of the town, but in the context of the illness and deaths that were gripping the town, increasing numbers of people began to blame the council for the disaster that had befallen them. An emergency meeting of the Town Council was called to 'consider the whole question of the recent epidemic' and to ensure 'that exaggerations might be met by accurate facts.'[16] It was hard to see how the gravity of the situation could be exaggerated, and the pressure on senior councillors continued to mount. Professor Crookshank wrote to the press, contradicting the mayor's assertion that he had known that his report would be suppressed. At the end of the month, it was reported that Patching had left Worthing, apparently because his health had 'given way.' Whether or not this was indeed the real reason, the *West Sussex Gazette* commented that it was 'a source of infinite regret' that the mayor should be absent 'at such a critical period in the history of the town.'[17]

There is good reason to believe that the anger of the town was not limited to indignant letters in the local newspapers. Mrs. Edith Anderson, who was 13 at the time of the epidemic recalled that 'the mayor and councillors had a very rough time [and] their houses had to be boarded up as the men were very angry.'[18] As we shall see, this anger did not abate and was very apparent towards the close of the year. The focal point for the town's indignation was Dr Goldsmith, who, as a medical man and a former local politician, was ideally placed to be a credible opposition to Patching, Churcher and their colleagues. In February 1893, Goldsmith had proposed a Worthing Ratepayer's Association, to challenge council policies.[19] At 'an enthusiastic meeting' later the same month, Goldsmith was elected president of the association.[20] So it is clear that he was already preparing for battle with the town authorities before the fever struck. Not all the members of the existing council were to be tarred with the same brush, however. There was much praise for Councillor Linfield and his brother, who, while other councillors had quit the town or were cowering behind boarded windows, was busy conveying the sick to one of the many temporary hospitals in the town. It was said that the Linfield brothers could be 'seen at all hours of the day' going about their charitable endeavours.[21]

The Worthing Dispensary and Infirmary had moved to new premises in Lyndhurst Road in 1882. It had three small wards, one each for men, women and children and these were soon full. Large tents were erected in the grounds to take new patients, yet still there was not enough room. Temporary hospitals were established throughout the town, including the Reading Rooms at Tarring and Broadwater. Mr G A Ralli donated a large house on Marine Parade as a temporary hospital.[22] It was noted that whereas all the patients in the 'Ralli Hospital' recovered, nearly 30% of the patients at the Infirmary died, such comparisons did little to help the already tarnished reputation of the town council. The subsequent report by Dr Kelly, published the following year, also raised the possibility that it was the moving of patients from their homes to hospitals that may have hastened their deaths, as moving them in their already exhausted state was more than they could bear. Later in the summer, nurses on bicycles were sent across Worthing to tend the sick in their homes.[23] One reason for removing patients was so that they would not infect other members of the household, another reason concerned the boiling of water. All householders were told to scald milk and to boil water for 15 minutes. This meant that during an exceptionally hot summer, fires were being lit while patients with very high fevers languished in bed. The introduction of static and mobile water tanks across the town, supplied with uncontaminated water, answered this problem but, as with so much of public policy at the time, the question was asked 'why did it take so long?' It brought relief for Edith Anderson and her family, who recalled: '.... the water carts came round, ringing a bell [and] we would rush out with jugs and kettles, "oh for freshwater.'[24]

▲ *Many died in Orme Road, a working-class district of the town (WSP).*

Children are at greater risk of contracting typhoid than adults as their immune system is still developing; however, mortality among children who are infected is usually lower than that in adults. The evidence from log books kept by head teachers in Worthing at the time seems to bear this out.[25] Christ Church School, in Portland Road, was in the heart of the most infected part of town. On 29th May, it was recorded that Rose May was 'very ill' with typhoid fever, but she does appear to have recovered. Her family lived in a very poor part of town. By 1901, she and her sister Ada had moved to South Norwood, where they were both working as domestic servants. However, the school log book entry for July 7th 1893 reports 'a great many' children absent, not just with typhoid but also whooping cough. Three days later it was reported that pupils John Street and Frank Hobbs were gravely ill with the fever.[26]

The school closed for the summer holidays on July 12th. When it reopened on August 14th, only 45 children, less than half the school, were present. Three days later the head teacher recorded the sad news that Kate Dunn had died and that 'she was a quiet and intelligent child and one of the brightest in her class.' On August 21st, there is a note that Edith Brazier has leave of absence to attend the funeral of her sister, Florence. The Braziers lived at the Clifton Arms, Clifton Road, where father, David, was the publican. Their son, George, also became a publican, of The Globe in Newland Road. One of his daughters, Phyliss, did very well for herself and married into the wealthy and influential Jordan family, estate agents and auctioneers in Worthing. She lived to be 102 and died in Ferring in 2015, 122 years after her aunt had died of typhoid.[27]

Another town centre school, Holy Trinity, (which opened in 1885), also suffered during the typhoid epidemic, although there do not appear to have been any deaths. Even in its first year, the school inspector noted 'the prevalence of sickness in the district'. One of the last deaths from typhoid in the town was that of the vicar of Holy Trinity, the Rev Joseph Lancaster, on November 30th 1893. The school log book stated: 'our beloved vicar this day passed away.'[28]

There are many heart-rending stories from the summer of 1893. These included a mother, recovering in one of the hospitals, looking forward to seeing her children when she recovered, yet they had both died of the fever; or the young woman, who was visited daily by her husband, who then stopped visiting: no one dared tell the sickly woman that her husband had contracted the fever too and had died. There were even stories of midnight burials and of porters fleeing the main hospital, leaving the nurses to carry away those who had died in the night.[29] Yet there is perhaps no more moving account than that given by Mrs L K Lidbetter, whose elder sister (Ellen Broadbridge) was in service, working as a maid, to a family in Worthing – this appears in full at the beginning of chapter 3. Mrs Lidbetter was born shortly after her sister died, so her account is based on what her parents told her, yet her account would seem reliable.

Although some victims did die quickly, as she reported, there are also cases of patients suffering for weeks, even months. It was often exhaustion that killed them. Contemporary accounts also give testimony to the appalling gloom and despair that descended on the town. A journalist working for the fashionable, London-based, *Pall Mall Gazette*, lived in Worthing and has left us a vivid account on the town at the time:

> 'On returning to my home in Worthing last week, I found the town almost deserted, the tradesmen depressed, ruin before many of them, and the typhoid still raging... We went out into the once bright little town. There was panic in the air. Groups of persons stood here and there on the pavements talking of the fever and the water supply. Tanks filled with water from the West Worthing Waterworks were placed about the streets... many of the residents have fled, and there are no visitors. The richer shopkeepers may be able to tide over their losses. Who is to blame? In great measure the Corporation. Instead of stopping the water supply in the spring during the first outbreak of typhoid, their chief concern was to prevent the news of the fever spreading about lest it should prevent visitors coming to the town... and now for eight weeks, while the people are falling sick around them and the cemetery is being chocked with new-made graves, they have met to wrangle over the price they should pay for the West Worthing Waterworks, and to receive suggestions on sources where water might be brought by fresh mains to the town; but do nothing!'[30]

In early September, the *Christian Herald* described Worthing as being 'a city of the dead,' and that 'pretty villas have their shutters up and gates padlocked, while the grass grows rank and course over what should be well-kept lawns.'[31] One councillor invited in a water-diviner, a Mr. John Mullins (also spelt 'Mullens'), who identified potential fresh water outlets near Colonel Wisden's home, The Warren at Broadwater.[32] This last initiative, however well-meaning, appears to have been the last straw for one correspondent to the *Worthing Gazette* in August, who also commented on the mounting opinion in the town that the council should resign:

> '...more than a month ago it was found that [our] water was full of typhoid germs. They have wasted their time and exhausted the patience of the people, with feeble suggestions and childish disputes. They summoned a conjurer to their aid [the water diviner]... There has been a cry raised that these men should resign, and give place to others who are more competent and more capable. It may be a question whether it would be wise thus to change horses while crossing the river. But surely some very loud expression of indignation would be salutary.'[33]

That such a letter should have appeared in the *Gazette*, the most conservative newspaper, was a clear sign of how serious things were getting for the ruling group on the council. Perhaps the correspondent's call for a 'loud expression of indignation' rather than mass resignations, was seen as a positive comment in the context of the crisis then gripping the town. However, others in the town had no doubts as to what should happen. The Rev J Lancaster, vicar of Holy Trinity, called on the whole council to resign.[34] There was no precedent for such demands in Worthing's history, but then there had been no crisis like this one.

As the town council elections of November 1893 approached, there was much speculation as to what would transpire. In the event only two of the sitting councillors, then up for re-election, put themselves forward again. New candidates came forward and were elected, unopposed, such was the strength of feeling in the town. However, William Churcher had no intention of standing down, as the owner of the town's best-selling newspaper, he may have judged that he had the means to weather the storm. Also standing again was Councillor Walter, a popular figure in the town, not so closely associated with the inner group of Patching, Cook and Churcher. The town, depressed and exhausted, was in no mood for elections, but neither had it any wish to see these men returned unopposed. At the last moment, it was announced that Dr Goldsmith would contest the election, as would his colleague, the solicitor, Henshell Fereday.

The *Worthing Intelligencer* and its proprietor, Walter Paine, had no doubt as to whom the electors should support: 'The great question is, are we to go on as we have been going on for the past six months? Are we to be governed or misgoverned with the same results which the past season has produced?' It reminded its readers of the 'terrible consequences of mismanagement' that the town had witnessed, and warned that 'if these gentlemen are to be allowed to continue their present policy, the future of Worthing is hopeless indeed.'[35] The *Worthing*

▼ *Through the good offices of Edward Harrison – owner of Lyons Farm – a temporary supply of fresh water was made available to the town in late summer 1893 (WSP).*

Gazette enraged their opponents by publishing anonymous correspondence on their letters' page, attacking Fereday and Goldsmith. Churcher himself described Goldsmith's plans to provide work for the unemployed during the winter as being 'clap trap promises to provide employment at the ratepayer's expense'. Worse than this however, Henshall Fereday described receiving an 'obscene postcard'. which he alleged had been sent by one of Churcher's supporters. The election was turning very nasty indeed. The result of the election was a triumph for Goldsmith and a humiliation for Churcher, who came bottom of the poll with only 159 votes. Fereday failed to be elected, although he received considerably more votes than Churcher. For Walter Paine at the *Intelligencer*, the election was 'a striking vindication of the fearless and outspoken' views of Dr Goldsmith who had exposed a 'policy of suppression and evasion'.[36] It was also reported that, although re-elected, Councillor Walter 'suffered a great deal of hustling and abuse' from the crowd that had gathered to hear the result. It should be remembered that only ratepayers could vote at this time, and therefore many of the poorer people, who probably made up the majority of the crowd, were disenfranchised. Churcher left the count 'by the back way', but the mob followed him home and, according to the *Intelligencer* 'his house was surrounded by a menacing crowd', who were only kept in check by 'the presence of several police officers'.[37]

For its part, the *Gazette*, licking the wounds of its defeat, castigated its rival for gloating 'over the prospect of personal violence to the proprietor of this paper', and declaring its belief that more should be expected from a rival newspaper 'than a tacit approval of rowdyism', It concluded its observations by inferring that the owner of the *Intelligencer* dared not stand for election himself, concluding, 'it is a matter of opinion whether Mr Walter Paine, had he been able to obtain a nomination, would have polled even 159 votes in the ward in which he has spent his life.'[38] The feud between Paine and Churcher appears to have been very personal. Churcher, as a young man, had worked for Paine, and the younger man's decision, in partnership with French, to establish the *Gazette* in 1883 as a rival to the *Intelligencer*, must have rankled with his older, former employer. Politics also played its part, Paine was a Liberal, while Churcher was a Conservative and the founding president of the Worthing Conservative Association. In local affairs, Churcher was of the conservative faction and Paine of the progressive group. Rivalry had now descended into bitterness and rancour.

Worse was to come for "The Clique" of the old council. The Worthing Bonfire Society, which had been somewhat tamed since the riots of the mid-1880s, now resolved to march through the town and give expression to the pent-up anger of the common people of Worthing, whose influence through the ballot box was limited. Meeting at the Castle in Newland Road, they paraded to the Town Hall in South Street. The local newspapers give little indication of what took place that night, although the *Gazette* referred to the 'strong force of police' under the command of Superintendent Long that was on the streets that night. Had it not been for the reminiscences of Edith Anderson, we might never have known of the strength of feeling that pervaded the town. Mrs. Anderson was 97 years old when she recalled the events, with some minor grammatical modifications, these are her recollections, as she wrote them down in 1977:

> 'November was a terrible month [and] the bonfire boys and
> numerous others had a torch light procession meeting at the Town
> Hall. The chief rider was on a white horse [and] his attendants on
> horses rode through the town hoisting effigies of the mayor and

councillors. When they got back to the Town Hall the effigies were
set alight. Very few [people] went out, people were very frightened.
All the procession then had a huge bonfire on the beach.'[39]

In the past, the holding of the November 5th revels during the week of the local
elections may have played rather well for certain gentlemen in the town, who
had often proved successful in being able to persuade the poorer people that they
shared a common interest and often a common enemy. It must have been very
uncomfortable indeed for these people to find themselves projected as the enemy
and being forced to hide from angry gangs of youths and men, many of whom had
lost loved ones to the fever. Mrs. Anderson recalled that people dared not go out on
the streets after 6pm during those days. She also recalled having to wash in the sea,
as there was no water to bathe in at home. All classes suffered during 1893, indeed
the *Pall Mall Gazette* was of the opinion that more of 'the well-to-do class' had died
than was the case amongst 'their poorer neighbours'.[40] Although the subsequent
reports into the outbreak tend to contradict this, it is interesting that the supposed
land-grab that some claim took place following the typhoid was dependent on
deaths amongst the property-owning class of the town.

At the end of December, the new council elected from their number new aldermen.
Once again, the *Intelligencer* rejoiced in telling its readers that 'The Clique' had been
defeated.[41] The much-praised Councillor Linfield was one of those raised to the rank of
alderman. It is interesting, though, that both Frederick Patching and his close associate,
Robert Piper, retained their positions. Despite everything that had happened, some
men, through their business interests, their patronage, and one suspects, their strong
familial links in the town, were able to survive, even when their name was held in
contempt by much, if not most, of the town. Again, it must be remembered that most
people did not have a vote and could only register their protest on the streets. The
anger amongst ordinary people was very well articulated by a female reader of the *West
Sussex Gazette*, who while congratulating Councillor Goldsmith on his election, warned
him that he would be judged by his deeds rather than his words:

'We do trust you will be as outspoken in action as in speech. We
have been very long suffering for some time, but there is a limit,
and once the women of Worthing take action, which they will do,
woe betide those who let us loose (sic) our Easter season. You little
know, some of you, what many of us have been reduced to...'[42]

Also in November, James Gilham Davis, an accountant of 15, Ann Street, was
charged with sending the 'obscene postcard' to Henshell Fereday. In court, Fereday
read out the contents of the postcard, it having been ascertained 'that no females
were present'. The newspapers did not give all the lurid details, but they did refer to
comments in the postcard that condemned 'pettifogging lawyers', and told Fereday
to 'keep his writs to himself'. Witnesses came forward to identify the handwriting
on the postcard as being that of Davis, including one of his own employees.[43]
None of this was good news for Churcher or the conservative grouping. Within a
year, Churcher would be dead, aged only 39. The *Gazette* declared that he had been
suffering from 'a striking complication of diseases'.[A] It also revealed that he had
lost both his wife and five-year-old daughter to typhoid, something that the mob
who surrounded his home the previous year must have been aware of. Churcher's

---

[A] *The death certificate for William Frederick Churcher shows he died at 35, Chapel Road on October 28th 1894. Dr
Gostling recorded the causes of death as: Subacute Tubular Nephritis, Influenza 1 month, Broncho-Pneumonia 14 days
and Heart Failure 6 days.*

surviving children were now left without parents. Walter Paine did not attend the funeral, although William Paine did. Fereday, while not regretting Churcher's passing, did communicate his 'sincere sympathy for the orphan children'.[44]

The new council was quick to deliver. A Relief Fund raised nearly £9,000, which was distributed to all those who could demonstrate hardship and loss of income as a result of the fever. The Council applied for and were successful in securing a £36,000 loan from the Local Government Board for the construction of a reservoir and pumping station at Broadwater. The new facility, which could hold 2,250,000 gallons of water, as opposed to the 110,000 gallons of the old water tower, was opened by the Duke of Cambridge on April 26th 1897.[45] At the same time, the disposal of sewage was addressed. A new pumping station with holding-tanks was constructed, ensuring that all sewage was pumped out to sea, without the risk of it being brought back on the next tide. The century-long problem of sewers backing up and basements flooding was solved by this arrangement. Truly, the new council had lived up to its promises. Over the next few years, new departures from the old conservative position were adopted. Electric lighting was introduced into the town; the Infirmary and Dispensary was upgraded into Worthing Hospital, with new wards, better equipment and more staff; an isolation hospital was opened at Swandean; and, generally, the town council moved to being a provider of services.[46]

It appeared that the 'old guard' had been defeated. Or had they? There is evidence, nearly all of it gathered from the oral tradition, to suggest that some people in the town did very well out of the aftermath of fever

▲ *In 1894, opportunity was taken to relay sewers in many Worthing streets, including here in Montague Street – looking east near the junction with Graham Road and near the New Street chapel (WSP).*

year. As a child, I heard old people talk about the 'Forty Thieves' of Worthing, men who made a great deal of money out of dubious land and property acquisitions following the typhoid epidemic. During the 1980s, I interviewed some of these people, who were still alive, although then in advanced old age. Fred Long believed that certain townsmen had claimed 'squatters' rights' over land formerly belonging to owners who had died of the typhoid. He also alleged that, amongst others, 'Patching and Denton' had told tenants, where the landlord or landlady had died: 'in future you pay rent to our collectors.' He further claimed that these men and others, fenced off unclaimed land, then securing it as their own after seven years.[47] Gertrude Jillett made the same claims, and again named 'Denton' as one of the leading beneficiaries of this legal trick.[48] Mrs. Greenbat, talking of the acute suffering of Worthing people in 1893, added: 'On the other hand, some benefited by taking land and property, they were later known as the "Forty Thieves". As a matter of fact, I was recently talking to a man who has lived all his life in Worthing and he said to me, "remember the Forty Thieves?"'[49] Mr. Stanley even thought that the renaming of the Vintners Arms as the 'Thieves Kitchen' was reference to the shady practices of those times.[50]

So, what are we to make of these allegations and of the curiously exotic-sounding conspiracy of the Forty Thieves? One thing is for sure, the description was in general usage before 1893. When Dr Goldsmith was elected a councillor, he resigned his position as president of the Worthing Ratepayers Association and was replaced by Mr F E Ovenden, who was himself elected to the council some years later. In a letter

to the *Worthing Intelligencer*, shortly after his election, he berated, not just the old council, but its predecessor, the Worthing Local Board: 'Thirty years ago the old Local Board went by the name of the Forty Thieves. They had a high old time of it, made money by the hatful, so it is said, and they could afford to be generous.'[51] Leaving, aside, for a moment the curious assertion that 'they could afford to be generous', it is worth noting Ovenden's caveat 'so it is said'. which he may have felt protected him from accusations of defamation; although his time limit of 'thirty years ago', just about ruled out anyone still serving on the local authority.

The following week, Alderman Robert Piper, a leading conservative, thought it prudent to reply to Ovenden, but in a manner that was as intriguing as it was unexpected: 'I see that Councillor Ovenden says the old Local Board went by the name of the "forty thieves". Is he not mixing up the Local Board with the Society of which our old friend Sir (sic) James Baker was president, and of whose hospitality, Mr Editor, you and I have often partaken in the old days...?'[52] James Baker was a man who was very much a local celebrity and seemed to become involved in just about every controversy that arose in the town over 40 years. Most notably, Baker led the campaign to drive the progressive Owen Breads out of Worthing. What is very interesting is that in those days, 1869, Walter Paine was a rival of Breads', whose *Fashionable Visitor's List* was, at that time, the only other newspaper in the town to rival the *Intelligencer*. Is it reading too much into Robert Piper's assertion that he had shared the hospitality of the 'forty thieves' with 'you', 'Mr Editor', as being a none too subtle hint that Paine himself had once held different allegiances to the ones he now championed?

In an obituary published following James Baker's death in 1903, it states that 'his fellow tradesmen highly esteemed him, and he was a prominent figure at the social assembly known as "The Forty Thieves", which held its social gatherings at the Marine Hotel.'[53] An innocent dining club – no more than a convivial gathering of old friends? Quite possibly. Yet one is forced to ponder further. How was it that Shoemaker James Baker was able to be so generous a benefactor to the poor of Worthing? To organise and presumably pay for lavish processions and firework displays must have been a costly business. How did he finance the cheap meat he secured for the town's poor and the free bread he distributed from his van to the people in Chapel Fields? Perhaps it all came from the money raised by the Forty Thieves, acting as a charitable institution? However, there was a long protracted legal case in Worthing, involving James Baker that raises some interesting questions. Over a number of years, descendants of John Markwick, a landowner in Worthing in the early 1800s, claimed that Baker had illegally taken possession of land rightfully theirs. In the late 1870s, John Markwick had actually secured compensation of £400, in an out-of-court settlement, for land that he claimed the Local Board had illegally taken possession of from the estate of his ancestor. In March 1893, the 'Markwick Claim' against James Baker was finally settled by Lord Justice A L Smith in Baker's favour. It was stated that 'Mr Baker's right to the property he had purchased in 1865 from those who had bought it forty years earlier being thoroughly established.'[54] Was this the basis for one of Owen Breads' slanders in 1869? And who else had benefitted from land dealings of 'forty years earlier'? One thinks of Councillor Ovenden's assertion that 'they made money by the hatful' and that 'they

◀ Alderman James G Denton twice served as mayor of Worthing (WSP).

could afford to be generous'. James Baker was famously generous and much loved in the town, but one is still left wondering at the wealth of a shoemaker, just as one is left wondering about the wealth of a councillor of another generation, also noted as a great benefactor, the grocer and twice mayor of Worthing – Alderman Denton.[B]

Of all the people I interviewed in the 1980s, none could be said to have had an intimate knowledge of the business dealings of those they referred to as the Forty Thieves, in particular Patching, Denton, and the town clerk, William Verrall. Those who are successful and wealthy in life are often looked on with envy by others who have not achieved their material gains. Equally, it seems unlikely that those I interviewed should have invented spurious claims, so long after the events they described, or that they should have all told the same story about the same individuals, unless there was some basis in fact in what they were saying. However, one lady I interviewed was from an upper middle-class family, and, furthermore, a family alleged to have been associated with the Forty Thieves. Lois Jordan was the granddaughter of Herbert Jordan, the man who had warned of a typhoid epidemic in 1888. Members of her family died in the outbreak, including her grandmother. Miss Jordan told me that her grandmother had wished to make a will with her own solicitor, Mr Gray, but instead it was Verrall, the town clerk, who wrote out the document. Miss Jordan said that her grandmother kept asking, in regard to the will, 'has Mr Gray seen it?' Miss Jordan did not believe that Mr Gray, despite her grandmother's wishes, was ever involved.

Miss Jordan was forthright in her opinion that several prominent townspeople were engaged in dishonest conduct in the aftermath of the typhoid epidemic, including members of her own family: 'My father talked of them grabbing land for nothing; then claiming Squatters' Rights. If you had the land for seven years you could claim it as yours. It's disgusting what under-handed men would do for money.'[55] She also explained how her uncle was the Grand Master of the local lodge of Freemasons: 'He told my father, "you join it and it will be good for business."' One wonders if the 'Forty Thieves' gatherings at the Marine Hotel in the 1860s had any connection or association with Freemasonry. The most extraordinary part of my interview with Miss Jordan came when she related an incident that happened to her one day, while out on an excursion to the Black Rabbit, near Arundel. She recalled how they got talking with a 'chalk worker', who 'became friendly with us'. The man then asked the girls' names: 'When we said "Jordan", he said, "I don't want to know you. You're one of the Forty Thieves."' A remarkable testimony, and one that sheds a chink of light on a very murky chapter in Worthing's history.

The struggle in the town between progressives and conservatives did not end with the elections of 1893. Five years later, there appears to have been a covert attempt by some councillors to oust the mayor, Captain Fraser, by putting up Edwin Lephard, a business associate of the Paine family, as a candidate against Fraser in his own ward.[56] There was a convention in those days that the mayor was always elected unopposed. In 1901, Ovenden was elected mayor, an apparent set-back for the conservative grouping, although it would be too easy to over-state the division between conservatives and progressives – there were no political groupings on the council in the modern sense and all candidates stood as independents. It was during Ovenden's mayoralty, in the summer of 1902, that the religious agitation of Peter

▲ *Lois Jordan as a young girl with her mother and brother on the beach near Splash Point (CH).*

[B] *Denton remains a fascinating and elusive character: a grocer who owned two shops, lived quite modestly, yet left a fortune on his death. His origins were very humble, he was also illegitimate – a great social handicap in those days, yet he rose to be the town's most esteemed citizen – surely a study for an up and coming local historian to explore in more detail?*

Woods provoked the ugliest scenes seen on the streets of Worthing since the Skeleton Army riots.[C] It is interesting that Peter Woods should have singled out a 'medical man' at the Anglo-Catholic St. Andrew's Church for criticism. Dr Goldsmith was a noted supporter and significant member of the congregation at St. Andrew's. He had strangely left Worthing only a year after his sensational election victory in 1893, returning to the town in February 1901.[57] One wonders if his enemies in the town were behind Woods' attacks; one also wonders if his death the following year, in July, was hastened by the controversy. Goldsmith of course had friends in the town, including his old colleague, Ovenden, who had directed the police to arrest Woods.

The election of Edward Patching as the chairman of the town's new Education Committee in 1903 showed that his star was undimmed, despite the events of ten years earlier. Indeed, Patching was re-elected as mayor in 1910 and served for two terms. Patching's close colleague, Robert Piper, was re-elected mayor in 1912, also serving two terms and was a key figure in the 'Worthing Police Scandal' of 1914, as indeed was Patching himself. The tussle between a progressive and conservative vision for the town continued. At a by-election in 1913, Alderman Linfield, who served as mayor from 1906-1908, was opposed by Paul Schweder of Courtlands, who rigorously opposed a number of progressive proposals, supported by Linfield, including the construction of a rubbish incinerator and the laying of a gas main to Goring. The election generated considerable interest, including allegations of intimidation on the part of local youths. Cars were used to ferry electors to the polling stations. Linfield was returned with a majority of 18 votes.[58] Astonishingly, some 76% of the electorate voted, higher than the turnout for some general elections in Worthing, for example, and way beyond turnout in any recent local elections in the town. Linfield's interest in politics continued after the war and in 1924 he was elected as a Liberal MP for Bedfordshire.[59] Denton, the protégé of Patching and Piper, was elected mayor for two successive years in 1908 and 1910, and again in 1922, during which year he was granted the Freedom of the Borough of Worthing.[60] He is remembered today for his numerous bequests to the town, including Denton Gardens and the Assembly Hall.

One matter regarding the typhoid epidemic should be clarified. It has been stated on several occasions that Dr Kelly, the medical officer, took his own life shortly after the epidemic. This was not the case and Dr Kelly remained the town's medical officer until his death in 1904.

Author's Note: readers wishing to know more about the scandalous and riotous proceedings from the Victorian era alluded to in this article may like to read my book, *Worthing in the Bad Old Days – Riot, Beer, and the Word of God.* For more information about Owen Breads and James Baker, please see my book, *Worthing, A History,* and *Worthing the Untold Story* (although now out of print, copies are available to borrow from Worthing Library).

[C] *'Worthing Excelsior Skeleton Army' (The Skeletons) formed from the ranks of the Bonfire Club, violently opposed the Salvation Army marching through their areas. Riots ensued and, when the Skeletons attacked the Police, Lt Col Wisden read the Riot Act from the steps of the Town Hall on August 20th 1884 and 40 mounted Dragoons from Preston Barracks helped restore order.*

1 *Phillipp's Hand-Book and Directory of Worthing (Worthing 1850), p.5*

2 *Hare, Chris. Worthing, A History Chapters 2 & 3 (2008)*

3 *Breads, Owen. 'New Guide and Hand-Book to Worthing' (Worthing 1859), p.17*

4 *Worthing Monthly Record, May 1st 1854*

5 *Virgoe, J M. 'Typhoid in Worthing in 'Fever Year' 1893'. The Local Historian, August 2006, pp. 163–174*

6 *Worthing Gazette, May 13th 1886*

7 *Worthing Gazette, January 23rd 1889*

8 *Worthing Intelligencer, May 10th 1890*

9 *Virgoe, ibid.*

10 *Virgoe, ibid.*

11 *Virgoe, ibid.*

12 *West Sussex Gazette, July 20th 1893*

13 *West Sussex Gazette, June 22nd 1893*

14 *Virgoe, ibid.*

15 *Virgoe, ibid.*

16 *West Sussex Gazette, July 20th 1893*

17 *West Sussex Gazette, July 27th 1893*

18 *West Sussex Record Office (WSRO), room 1, shelf 37c4, Box V, ref:MP 1390*

19 *Worthing Intelligencer, February 4th 1893*

20 *Worthing Intelligencer, February 18th 1893*

21 *The War Cry, July 26th 1893*

22 *West Sussex Gazette, July 27th 1893*

23 *Kelly, Charles. 'Report on the Epidemic of Enteric Fever in 1893 in the Borough of Worthing, in Broadwater and in West Tarring'. (Brighton 1894)*

24 *WSRO ibid.*

25 *Hare, Chris. https://southdownsgenerations.org.uk/sickness-and-mortality-in-south-down-schools/ Both the Christ Church and Holy Trinity log books are kept at West Sussex Record Office, WSRO, WSRO/E/218N.*

26 *Ibid, this information comes from the Christ Church Infants' School logbook, WSRO, E218F/12/1, Mary Mckeown has established that both these children survived into adulthood, although Frank Hobbs was killed in 1916 during the Great War.*

27 *The author is indebted to Phil Wood for his genealogical website family history research on these typhoid victims.*

28 *Holy Trinity Infant School log book, WSRO, E218N/12/1*

29 *Sussex Daily News, August 16th 1893*

30 *Pall Mall Gazette, August 18th 1893*

31 *Christian Herald, September 7th 1893*

32 *West Sussex Gazette, August 20th 1893*

33 *Worthing Gazette, August 16th 1893*

34 *Ibid.*

35 *Worthing Intelligencer, October 28th 1893*

36 *Worthing Intelligencer, November 4th 1893*

37 *Ibid.*

38 *Worthing Gazette, November 8th 1893*

39 *WSRO, ibid.*

40 *Pall Mall Gazette, August 24th 1893*

41 *Worthing Intelligencer, December 23rd 1893*

42 *West Sussex Gazette, November 9th 1893*

43 *Worthing Intelligencer, November 18th 1893*

44 *Worthing Gazette, October 31st 1894*

45 *Migeod, F W H (ed). 'Worthing: A survey of Times Past and Present' (Worthing 1938), pp 188–196*

46 *Ibid.*

47 *Notes of interview by the author in his possession.*

48 *Ibid.*

49 *Ibid.*

50 *Ibid.*

51 *Worthing Intelligencer, February 5th 1898*

52 *Worthing Intelligencer, February 12th 1898*

53 *Worthing Gazette, July 15th 1903*

54 *Worthing Intelligencer, March 4th 1893*

55 *Notes of interview with Miss Jordan in the possession of the author.*

56 *Worthing Intelligencer, October 29th 1898*

57 *Worthing Gazette, July 29th 1903*

58 *Worthing Mercury, March 8th 1913*

59 *Worthing Gazette, August 6th 1924*

60 *Worthing Herald, January 13th 1923*

Chapter 3
A Better Way

Assembled by Colin Reid

In the previous chapter, Chris Hare gave a telling description of those leaders whose conduct fell short during the typhoid epidemic, leading to much 'bitterness and recrimination'. However, mercifully, that was only part of the picture – there were many examples of human kindness, of people who acted with integrity and sacrificiously.

Who can fail to be moved by the story of Ellen Broadbridge and her family?

> 'My parents, George and Olive Broadbridge lived in the village of Washington, seven miles out. My parents fetched my little sister home from Worthing in what was called the "Carriers Cart", then [my father] carried her nearly a mile in his arms home, only to die three weeks later. My father never really got over the death as she was his first born. And now the district nurse came and ordered all the bedding to be burnt outside in the garden, and stayed till my father did what she told him to... Everything that my sister laid on was burnt too, my mother said it was a very distressing time and left them very poor, as my father worked very hard but not much wages in those days. During the time she was alive, my father walked there and back the seven miles each way to get ice for my sister to suck. But he said the people died very quickly as there was insufficient medical help to nurse them and those that had fever in the home had to put a card on the doors to forbid people to go in or out and tradespeople would leave food on the doorstep. And the same applied for the undertakers to come at dark to fetch the dead out, and at the worst time they had to dig a long trench and they were buried side by side. This is somewhere in Broadwater Cemetery.'*

In a letter dated January 23rd 1977[1] from 79-year-old Mrs Laura Lidbetter writing in response to an appeal for information about the typhoid epidemic and a sound recording.

Note: Ellen and her older sister, Flora Jane, had been born illegitimately to Olive Richardson. Her birth had been registered as Ellen Louisa Richardson in Thakeham district in 1879, a few months before her mother married George Broadbridge. He was an agricultural labourer from Wiston and they set up home in the Springs and then Pigland areas of Olive's home village, Washington. Sometime after 1891, Ellen left home and found employment as a servant to the Stubbs fishmonger family in Worthing. She was only 14 years old when she died at home in Washington on August 15th 1893. She was laid to rest the next day in the parish churchyard of St Mary's.

George Broadbridge died on August 19th 1915 and was buried on August 23rd in an extension to the churchyard across the road from St Mary's Church, and his widow, Olive, died on October 13th 1931 and was buried in the same grave as her husband.

This is a striking example but – given the hundreds of people, who became infected with typhoid – there will have been countless examples of kindness by family, extended family and friends. In this chapter we will hear stories of professionals such as doctors, nurses and teachers who became infected with typhoid and died but, as referred to by Chris Hare, this chapter begins with an account of the Linfield brothers whose conduct was exemplary.

▲ *St Mary's Church, Washington circa 1900 (CR).*

THE LINFIELD BROTHERS
(By Malcolm Linfield)

Some of my grandfather's earliest memories went back to 'fever year' in Worthing, when he recalled how his father drove around in a horse-drawn cab, carrying blankets and helping to convey patients from their homes to one of the temporary hospitals. Arthur George Linfield (junior) was born in August 1885, eldest son of Arthur George and Edith Mary Linfield. He also remembered being sent by his mother to fetch clean water from one of the portable water tanks because the mains supply was polluted. He said it was the example of his father, who devoted much of his life to the poor, which inspired him to engage in social work.[2]

In 1893, the family were renting a house in North Street which was just round the corner from High Street where one of the portable water tanks was located. This would have been the one where eight-year-old Arthur took his jug, close to the Swan Inn (Fig. 1). In his long life of 88 years, Arthur actively supported a number of local organisations which included Worthing Hospital, Gifford House (the Queen Alexandra Home for Disabled Servicemen, now called Care for Veterans) and the Worthing Council of Social Service (now Guild Care), of which he was one of the founders.

Arthur's father and his two uncles all played their part during the typhoid epidemic. Their parents, William and Anne Linfield, came to Worthing from Surrey soon after their marriage at Brighton in 1850. William was a master tailor by

▶ *Fig. 1: The water tank in High Street where Arthur would have fetched fresh water for his family. The temporary hospital at The Hollies can be seen at the top of the street (WSP).*

trade and saw the potential which Worthing offered, setting up in business at 2, South Place, near the old Town Hall. His marriage to Anne Caesar produced three sons and two daughters. Their sons were **William Henry Linfield (1854–1924)** who became relieving officer in the service of the East Preston Guardians and also Registrar of births and deaths; **Arthur George Linfield (1859–1938)**, a Worthing fruit grower, and long-serving member on the board of the East Preston Guardians; and their youngest son, **Frederick Caesar Linfield (1861–1939)**, a well-known local businessman and politician who became one of the first councillors when Worthing was incorporated in 1890 (see Family Tree below).

All three brothers were motivated by a strong faith and it was their firm commitment to Christian values which explains the way they responded during the typhoid epidemic. Interestingly, though brought up in the Church of England, two of them gravitated towards Methodism. Arthur was attracted to the Wesleyan Methodists, and worshipped at the chapel in Bedford Row, whilst his younger brother Frederick joined the Primitive Methodists and worshipped at the Iron Chapel in Chapel Road, prior to its removal to Lyndhurst Road in 1893 when the new Primitive Methodist Chapel was built. They all had a strong social conscience, which was inseparable from their profound religious beliefs.

▼ *Fig. 2: Linfield Family Tree.*

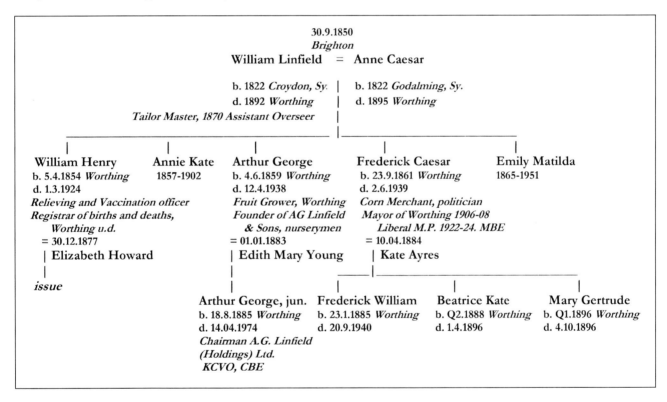

30.9.1850
Brighton
William Linfield = Anne Caesar

b. 1822 *Croydon, Sy.* | b. 1822 *Godalming, Sy.*
d. 1892 *Worthing* | d. 1895 *Worthing*
Tailor Master, 1870 Assistant Overseer |

William Henry — **Annie Kate** — **Arthur George** — **Frederick Caesar** — **Emily Matilda**

b. 5.4.1854 *Worthing* — 1857-1902 — b. 4.6.1859 *Worthing* — b. 23.9.1861 *Worthing* — 1865-1951
d. 1.3.1924 — d. 12.4.1938 — d. 2.6.1939
Relieving and Vaccination officer — *Fruit Grower, Worthing* — *Corn Merchant, politician*
Registrar of births and deaths, — *Founder of AG Linfield* — *Mayor of Worthing 1906-08*
Worthing u.d. — *& Sons, nurserymen* — *Liberal M.P. 1922-24. MBE*
= 30.12.1877 — = 01.01.1883 — = 10.04.1884
| Elizabeth Howard — | Edith Mary Young — | Kate Ayres
|
issue

Arthur George, jun. — **Frederick William** — **Beatrice Kate** — **Mary Gertrude**
b. 18.8.1885 *Worthing* — b. 23.1.1885 *Worthing* — b. Q2.1888 *Worthing* — b. Q1.1896 *Worthing*
d. 14.04.1974 — d. 20.9.1940 — d. 1.4.1896 — d. 4.10.1896
Chairman A.G. Linfield
(Holdings) Ltd.
KCVO, CBE

Arthur George Linfield (1859–1938)

Arthur Linfield was one of the pioneering glasshouse growers in the town,

originally having a small market garden with greenhouse near the Worthing Infirmary. He had a greengrocer's shop in Warwick Street where he sold his produce. However, in 1884 he had much greater ambitions, and took on four acres which he leased from Robert Piper to the east of Ham Lane where he started to build some substantial greenhouses. He eventually had several nurseries in the East Worthing area, the main crops being tomatoes, grapes and cucumbers. Mushrooms were also grown from the earliest days, mainly as a catch-crop beneath

◀ *Fig. 3: Arthur George Linfield, c1893 (ML).*

▲ *Fig. 4: Arthur Linfield in North Street with three of his children, c1893. The boy on the right is his eldest son, Arthur jun., born in 1885 (ML).*

the grape vines and Arthur made a speciality of growing them. Over time, Arthur was joined in the business by his five sons and in 1913 an old dairy farm was bought at Thakeham to provide work for the younger children.

In 1893, Arthur was 34 years old; it was also the year when he was first elected to the board of the East Preston Guardians. As well as the Town Council, the East Preston Guardians were responsible for setting up a number of temporary hospitals because the Worthing Infirmary was too small to cater for the large numbers falling ill. Arthur was appointed to the sub-committee[A] 'to secure and fit up as temporary hospitals, the St. Georges Mission Room, the Training Home in High-street and the Primitive Methodist Iron Chapel in Lyndhurst Road'.[3] These buildings enabled accommodation for another 96 patients, the objective being the need to isolate all suspected cases by removing them from their homes. The Poor Law Medical Officers, Mr Opie and Mr Nodes, provided medical attendance with their respective assistants across the three buildings, assisted by ten trained nurses which the East Preston Guardians gave orders to employ.

The 'Training Home' at the top end of High Street, formerly known as North End Cottage, was used as a training school for servants. Now called 'The Hollies', this late eighteenth-century villa was built in the local yellow brick, and features in the background of the most evocative photograph taken during the epidemic which shows one of the galvanised tanks of drinking water. Arthur often attended to the sick and dying, personally visiting the poorer homes, especially in the north-east ward, and then carrying out the patients to be brought back to this building for medical care. He also turned his own house into accommodation for some of the nurses.[4] Two contemporary photographs passed down through the family show the medical staff with some of their patients taken in front of 'The Hollies', including Arthur and his younger brother Frederick (Fig. 6).

Arthur remained a Guardian at East Preston for the next 37 years, right up until the Poor Law Unions were abolished in 1930 and poor relief administration transferred

▶ *Fig. 5: Arthur Linfield in one of his vineries in Ham Lane, with a catch crop of mushrooms growing on the floor, c.1894/95 (ML).*

[A] *The sub-committee of Guardians appointed to secure and fit-up the temporary hospitals included Mrs Gresson, Mr Melvill Green, Captain A B S. Fraser, Mr M King, Mr H . Gardner, Mr G Beer and Mr A G Linfield.*

to local government. He was elected as chairman in 1925 and at their final meeting, William Sams, the senior member and vice-chairman, made a speech in which he paid tribute to their chairman, referring to the year he was first elected as 'a very critical one in the history of Worthing'.[5] He remembered 'the good work he did at the time in conjunction with another respected member of the Board, the late Mr Michael King, of Broadwater'. He described Arthur as a 'first-rate worker, progressive and humanitarian' who had also 'given freely of his means as well as his advice'.

In the religious life of Worthing, Arthur was regarded as a 'highly esteemed worker at the Steyne Gardens Methodist Church'.[6] His son recalled that 'he devoted a lot of his life to work for the poor, and he was also a very good Christian, which set me a good example as a boy'.[7] In the early 1880s, before the Methodist Church was built in Tarring Road, Arthur would visit the site of the building and preach the gospel. A plaque on the wall outside commemorates the fact that Arthur Linfield 'preached from this site' at a time when Methodism was emerging in Worthing as an evangelical force. On January 1st 1883, he married Edith Mary Young[8] at the Wesleyan chapel in Bedford Row. (Edith who came from a well-known Methodist family in Lancing.) They had five sons and two daughters; sadly, their son Harold was killed in action during the First World War.

Arthur was very keen on spreading the Methodist message and was heavily involved in building new churches to facilitate this. The Wesleyan Chapel at Ashington was built in 1894, and – to cater for an expanding congregation – Arthur played a major role in the building of the new Wesleyan Church at Steyne Gardens, which opened in 1900 and superseded the old chapel in Bedford Row. During his life, he had filled all the offices within his church, but what he loved most, according to one commentator, was 'to make life a little happier for people'.[9] In 1933, he was presented with an illuminated scroll to celebrate his golden jubilee as a local preacher. Arthur died in 1938 at the age of 79.

▲ *Fig. 6: This is one of the two contemporary photographs taken outside the front of the temporary hospital at The Hollies' set up by the East Preston Guardians in 1893. It depicts medical staff, including the doctors and nurses, with some of their patients. Councillor Frederick Linfield is standing in the middle row with his arms folded, whilst his brother Arthur is seated on the right of the photograph (ML).*

William Henry Linfield (1854–1924)

Arthur's older brother, William Henry Linfield, was a relieving officer at Worthing, in the service of the East Preston Guardians. He was also later appointed vaccination officer and after the death of Robert Gravett in 1902, he succeeded him as registrar of births and deaths. William married Elizabeth Howard in 1877[10] at the parish church in Chawton, near Southampton, and they moved to Lyndhurst Road in 1881. They had nine children in total, three boys and six daughters. He also owned a small nursery, which was attached to the family home, with a number of glasshouses in which he grew tomatoes and other early-season produce for which Worthing was nationally famous. He employed a foreman, William Mariner, to manage the nursery for him. William frequently attended court proceedings in pursuit of his various duties and as such his name often appears in the local newspapers. During 'fever year,' William was often seen helping to fetch the sick from their homes and taking them to one of the temporary hospitals, as this extract from 'The War Cry' reveals:

> 'Councillors Frazer and Butcher superintend the distribution of pure water, Councillor FC Linfield, with his brother, Relieving Officer Linfield, can be seen at all hours of the day, conveying the failing sick to one of the many hospitals. That their hearts are in their work, can be seen, by their gentleness as they carry the young in their arms, and by their attention and kindness to the elder ones as they are borne to their destination on stretchers'.[11]

It had been found in the early days of the fever that many patients were fatally injured by the rough manner in which they were conveyed during the 'ambulance work,' so William and Frederick were keen to make the journey as calm and comfortable as possible.

However, during the first outbreak of the fever, William became very ill and was unable to carry out any of his duties as relieving officer. For someone who prided himself in his devotion to duty and apparently never took a single day's holiday during the whole of his 40 years of service to the East Preston Guardians,[12] it must have been fairly serious. In the Board minutes of June 13th 1893,[13] the clerk alluded to the inconvenience of R O Linfield's continued illness because the weekly returns could not be submitted to the Local Government Board. Capt. Hills proposed that Mr Gibbs be appointed to keep the books for Worthing No 2 district until William had recovered. It was then proposed by Capt. Hills that Mr E A Plummer be appointed 'temporary substitute for R O Linfield' and that the Local Government Board be informed.

On July 11th 1893, a letter was read to the Guardians sanctioning the temporary arrangements for the administration of relief in the Worthing district during R O Linfield's illness. Although there is no implicit reference as such, but bearing in mind that William was indisposed for several weeks before he was once again available to work at the Relief Office, it is not unreasonable to assume that he had succumbed to typhoid fever. His very unpleasant symptoms probably started with headaches, insomnia and feverishness, a gradually increasing temperature, accompanied by stomach pains and diarrhoea. These symptoms would intensify for a couple of weeks, and then, in most cases, a gradual recovery with a prolonged convalescence. Severe attacks could lead to death through exhaustion, internal bleeding and ulceration of the intestine.

Although some people thought of him as 'seemingly aloof', William was fully aware of the poverty around him. On one such occasion, for instance, seeing an old lady cleaning the step of a villa, he went up to her and suggested she come and see him at the Relief Office in the morning.[14] However, he was less sympathetic to a wayward cousin who briefly came to stay in Worthing and was hauled before the magistrates for her drunken behaviour. When she visited the Relief Office, William 'refused to own her' although she still received her 5 shillings.[B] William retired in 1920 and died at the age of 69 in 1924.

Frederick Caesar Linfield (1861–1939)

Whilst all three brothers faced considerable risk of catching the disease through close contact with infected persons, it was the youngest brother, Frederick Caesar Linfield, who apparently took the greatest risks. Frederick had been involved in local politics for a number of years, initially joining the old Local Board in 1888, and then being elected one of the first councillors when Worthing was incorporated in 1890, representing the north-east ward.[15] He was in business as a corn merchant, with premises in Chapel Road and Montague Street, and later added coal to his portfolio, which he saw as a sound business opportunity because of the significant quantities required by the local fruit growers. He married Kate Ayres at the Congregational Chapel in 1884[16] and they had two sons and two daughters. In 1893, Frederick was 32 and had just played a prominent role in the building of a new Primitive Methodist Church in Chapel Road; his daughter Beatrice, watched by the pupils of her Sunday school, laid the first foundation stone in August 1892.

During the typhoid epidemic, Frederick really rose to the occasion and did his utmost to help, which was in contrast to many of the local councillors who simply wanted to protect themselves and their families and left the town. He was involved with the discussions in his church to make the old Iron Chapel available as one of the new temporary hospitals, which soon had 36 beds available and a staff of nurses and doctors who had been recruited from London. However, it was the very active part he played, often in the company of one of his brothers, which inspired the most praise. He was reputed to have personally carried hundreds of victims to the ambulance in the street, but where he put himself in most danger was when he helped remove the dead from the hospitals. It was, to say the least, distressing work and he recalled the shocking experience of how on one occasion 'when he had hired a tramp from a lodging house to assist him in this work, he found on striking a match in the mortuary, he was in the presence of two other dead bodies.'[17] Since so many people had left the town, it made it much more difficult to deal with the emergency.

When it came to the municipal election, the voting public showed what they really felt about the council and its dismal management of the crisis. Most of the council either declined

◀ Fig. 8: Alderman Frederick Caesar Linfield (from the Primitive Methodist Magazine 1903).

▼ Fig. 9: Frederick Caesar & Kate Linfield with their two eldest children: Frederick William & Beatrice Kate circa 1892 (ML).

[B] *The relative, Emily Frances Linfield came to Worthing in the late 1890s to stay with her elderly mother in Warwick Road. It was William's daughter Ethel who saw her in the Relief Office and witnessed her father's reaction to her, as revealed in a family letter.*

to stand again or were defeated. Councillor Linfield's efforts during the crisis were rewarded with his promotion to alderman, notwithstanding his non-conformity, his radical politics and his youth. However, although he managed to avoid the disease despite the extensive exposure he faced, Frederick did suffer from the considerable strain of the epidemic and for the next four or five years he suffered a serious breakdown in his health.

For Frederick, the year 1896 was particularly difficult for him and his family. It was an *annus horribilis* in every sense, not only marred by Frederick's continuing health problems but the added pain of two family bereavements. In February, Frederick's wife gave birth to a baby girl, whom they named Mary Gertrude but, on April 1st 1896, Frederick and Kate sadly lost their elder daughter Beatrice at the age of seven from diphtheria,[18] a highly contagious bacterial infection to which Victorian children were particularly vulnerable. In May, on the advice of his physician, Frederick moved to the north of Scotland for several months to improve his health. The *Worthing Gazette* reported that he had 'been in impaired health for some months past, suffering from sleeplessness and loss of appetite, the results of a nervous disorder, which seems to have reached an acute stage, necessitating an entire cessation from active occupation, with complete rest and quiet'.[19]

Frederick returned to Worthing sometime before August 5th 1896, 'apparently much benefitted by his health-seeking journey to the Highlands',[20] and undoubtedly very pleased to be reunited with his family and to see his baby daughter again. However, his road to full recovery was seriously dented by Mary's death on October 4th from tubercular peritonitis.[21] She was 8 months old. Both sisters were buried in the cemetery in South Farm Road.

Frederick's continuing involvement in local politics eventually saw him twice become mayor of Worthing between 1906 and 1908. During his mayoralty, he took a keen interest in a scheme to extend Worthing Hospital, and it was largely through his efforts that £2,021 was raised to fund this.[22] He also had ambitions to get into Parliament, standing as a Liberal candidate for the division of Horncastle, Lincolnshire in December 1910, losing by only 524 votes.[23] In his business life, he made his eldest son Frederick William (FW) a partner in 1905. For a number of years, Frederick (FC) had also been developing an interest in land and property, which involved him buying up houses using multiple mortgages in various parts of Worthing. In 1911, his son bought his share in the corn and coal merchant's business, giving him more time to concentrate on his property development.

By 1914, Frederick owned a large part of the Heene estate which he was keen to develop. Unfortunately, though, the outbreak of war in August 1914 meant that he was unable to develop this land and could

▼ *Fig. 10: Local council election card for Frederick C. Linfield, for the north-east ward (ML).*

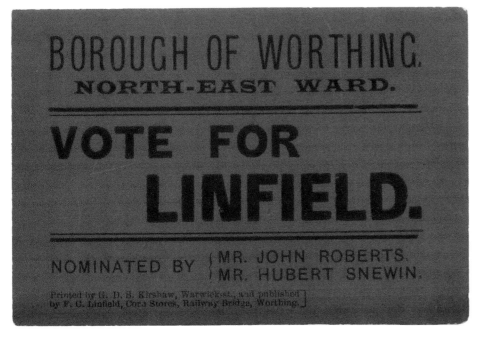

no longer service his mortgages. The outlook was grim and he soon found himself getting into serious financial difficulties, which ended up in the Brighton Bankruptcy Court. The final outcome was that he effectively had to hand over the whole of his property portfolio, and having made a composition under the Bankruptcy Act, from the date of approval he was disqualified from holding office as an alderman of the council. He eventually left Worthing to start a new life.

On May 20th 1915, his son FW put up his business for sale at auction and enlisted in the armed forces. FC wanted to pursue his career in politics, although with the war in full action, he initially took a job in the Ministry of Munitions Inventions Department, for which he was awarded an MBE. Once the war was over and their affairs had been concluded in Worthing, FW and his father decided to buy a house together in Huron Road, Balham which they could share.

In 1922, FC contested mid-Bedfordshire for the Liberals and finally achieved his long-held ambition of getting into Parliament. He was a particularly active MP, speaking on a wide range of issues in the Commons. Unfortunately for his political career, while he was away on a parliamentary commission in East Africa, a general election was called and he lost his seat. After his defeat, he took up the post of honorary secretary of the London Liberal Federation. He again contested mid-Bedfordshire in 1929 but was unsuccessful.

On February 8th 1929, his wife Kate died[24] and was buried in the Broadwater and Worthing Cemetery in South Farm Road. Frederick Caesar Linfield continued to live at Balham after his wife's death and died there on June 2nd 1939.[25] He was 77 and was also buried in Worthing.

THEY ALSO SERVED
Edith Emily Maria Hawksworth (By Mary Mckeown)

Edith was born in Wandsworth, very early in 1859, one of at least seven children born to William and Ann Hawksworth and she was baptised at All Saints' Church, Wandsworth on February 22nd. The baptismal register shows William as being a Gentleman, with the census record of 1861 showing his occupation as a bookseller of Paternoster Row in the City of London. By 1871, the family had moved to Eddington in Kent, where they were to live for many years. Edith's father, now 52 years old, had retired from his business.

Edith was still living with her family at the time of the 1881 Census. Although she was now 22 years old, it would appear she had not started her nursing career or had any other occupation. Her brother, Herbert, who was just 23 years old at that time was a surgeon and this may have influenced Edith to follow a nursing career. She commenced working at Sussex County Hospital in 1886, studied for certification between 1887 and 1888 and was registered on March 7th 1890.

Come the 1891 Census, Edith was living in Victoria Road, Worthing with the Lefevre Austin household, and was listed as a hospital nurse. At the time of her death, Edith was 34 years old and her address was given as Grafton Road, Worthing. She died on July 5th 1893 at the Infirmary after contracting typhoid whilst nursing. Edith was buried two days later in a brick-lined grave in Broadwater Cemetery. The following article[26] was published after her death:

> A KIND correspondent writes from Brighton:
>
> 'On July 5th died Sister EDITH HAWKSWORTH, Sister-in-Charge of the Sussex County Hospital Nursing Home. At her own urgent desire she left Brighton seven weeks ago, to help in nursing the poor of Worthing, during the recent outbreak of typhoid fever

there. After working hard for three weeks, seeing often 30 cases a day, she fell ill with the same fever and died on July 5th. She was buried on July 7th, in Worthing Churchyard, and was followed to her grave by many of the Nurses of the Sussex County Nursing Home. Sister HAWKSWORTH has been connected with the above Hospital since 1886, and her loss will be greatly felt, not only amongst the present set of Nurses at the Hospital Home, but amongst numbers of Nurses who started their Nursing career at the Sussex County Hospital.'

▼ The base of Edith's tombstone was surmounted by a cross before vandalism (MM).

The headstone on Edith's grave is one of only three headstones in Broadwater and Worthing Cemetery that refer in any way to the typhoid epidemic. Although, over the years, the inscription has worn, the following is still legible:

'IN LOVING MEMORY OF
EDITH
DAUGHTER OF THE LATE
WILLIAM HAWKSWORTH
OF EDDINGTON KENT
WHO DIED ON JULY – T--D FEVER
CONTRACTED WHILE NURSING AGED 34
SO HE BRINGETH THEM UNTO THE HAVEN
WHERE THEY WOULD BE PSALM CVII'

In chapter 4, there is a photograph of doctors and nurses outside The Travellers' Rest Temporary Hospital in Clifton Road. A nurse called Edith is seated second from left on the ground. Might this be Edith Hawksworth? We may never know.

Francis Westall Farrant (By Colin Reid):
Francis Westall Farrant was born on April 27th 1866 and baptised on July 17th 1866 at Llandudno, Caernarvonshire. He was the fourth of five children born to Robert Farrant and Mariana Reece, who had married in the district of Kings Norton in 1859. They set up home at Manville House, Llandudno and, in the 1861 Census, Robert is described as attorney, solicitor and lieutenant with the Rifles Volunteers born in the village of Clayhidon, Devon. His wife, Mariana, had been born on May 21st 1840 and when her parents – William Henry Reece (an attorney) and Maria – had her baptised in St Philip's Cathedral, Birmingham the family were resident in New Street.

Robert Farrant died at Llandudno on December 24th 1867, leaving an estate of £6,000. His widow, Mariana, never remarried and, for a while she continued in Llandudno but by 1881, she was residing in Albert Road, Great Malvern, Worcestershire. Her eldest, Robert Reece Farrant, took holy orders and became vicar of Welland, Worcestershire. She sent the younger sons, Henry, Francis and Percy to Repton School and then on to Oxford University where Francis initially studied at Trinity College whilst his two brothers were in New College. The following extract is taken from Oxford Men 1880 to 1892:[27]

'Farrant, Francis Westall, born at Llandudno, co. Carnarvon, 27 April 1866; 3s. Robert, gent. TRINITY, matric. 17 Oct., 85, aged 19 (from Repton school), scholar HERTFORD 85, B.A. and M.A. 92; HONOURS: - 3 classical mods. 87, 3 classics 89.'

On the 1891 Census, Francis Farrant was living with his mother and brothers at Heather Bank in the village of Welland, Worcestershire, where he was working as a tutor. Then, on December 7th 1892, he married Edith Watson Pike in Great Malvern and, shortly after that, they moved to Worthing where they lived at Belmont in Tennyson Road. On July 10th 1893, Francis died at home in Worthing of typhoid fever, which he had contracted three weeks earlier. In an article entitled 'Typhoid-Stricken Worthing', there is a reference to a conversation with the Rev. Lancaster, vicar of Holy Trinity, Worthing that clearly refers to Francis Farrant, although his name is not mentioned in the text:

Extracted from the Daily Graphic:[28]

'Another particularly pathetic case was that of a gentleman who had taken high honours at Hertford College, Oxford, and had invested all his capital in the purchase of a school for boys last December. He was married to a charming and clever young wife, and the two were building up a most flourishing scholastic connection. The fever broke out badly here, attacking several, one of whom has had a serious relapse, and is still lying ill, while the master himself died after a week's illness, leaving the poor widow, who expects her first baby in a few weeks, unprovided for.'

Francis had made a will and left an estate of over £1,200 to his widow Edith, who left the town and gave birth to their daughter, Edith May Farrant, in Great Malvern, Worcestershire on September 17th 1893. Subsequently, Edith and her daughter lived with Edith's parents in Ealing, Middlesex and in Margate, Kent.

Francis' father-in-law, Thelwell Pike, was present when Francis died, so it was probably he who arranged for Francis' body to be removed to Great Malvern burial ground for internment on July 14th.

Sarah Ellis (By Mary Mckeown):

Sarah was born on March 4th 1834 and baptized on August 31st 1834 in Portsea, Hampshire. She was the daughter of William and Sarah and had 4 siblings: William, Mary, Emma and George. Initially, their father was employed as a coal merchant in 1841 and by the 1851 Census he was a timber merchant employing 8 men. In about 1845 his wife, Sarah, died and he was left to raise his family alone.

In 1861, the family were living in Lion Terrace, Portsea. Sarah, now aged 27, is a governess while her younger sister Emma is a housekeeper. Ten years later, Sarah and Emma are now principals of a boarding school in Sheep Street, Winslow, Buckinghamshire. They have 17 female pupils, including their cousins Louisa, Clara and Susan Ellis. Their uncle, Samuel Ellis, is also resident, together with a cook and a domestic servant.

KINGSCLERE, LIVERPOOL GARDENS.

THE MISSES ELLIS

OFFER a thoroughly finished education to the daughters of private and professional gentlemen.

Resident French Governess (Parisienne).

Special arrangements can be made for the daughters of visitors.

Highest References, with Prospectus, on application.

By 1881, Sarah and Emma are principals of a school called 'Kingsclere' at 28, Liverpool Gardens, Worthing, with 12 pupils including their niece Louisa M Ellis aged 10 years. Then, 10 years later, Louisa is still at the school, having reached the position of school assistant. She is also joined by Grace A Ellis, another niece of Sarah and Emma's.

On July 21st 1893, Sarah died aged 59, from enteric fever. She had been ill for 28 days and she died at Kingsclere, Liverpool Gardens, Worthing with her sister Emma by her side. Sarah was buried on July 25th 1893 in Norwood Cemetery.

By 1901, Emma had moved from Worthing and was the principal of a school in Aldrington, Sussex. Assisting her at the school were her two nieces Louisa and Grace Ellis. Emma died in a nursing home in Worthing, aged 94 in 1937.

Dr William John Harris (By Colin Reid):

William John Harris was born on May 16th 1838 and was baptised at St Mary's Church, Broadwater on June 24th. He was the first son of William Harris, a surgeon, who hailed from Bovey Tracey, Devon, and Ellen, youngest child of the highly-regarded, Dr Michael Morrah of Warwick Hall, High Street, Worthing. William and Ellen married at St Mary's Church, Broadwater on May 3rd 1837 – a year before her father's death.

By the time of the 1841 Census, they were living at 24, High Street with their two sons: William John, and George. Also in the household was Ellen's 70-year-old widowed mother, Charlotte Morrah. Widowed in 1845, William married his second wife, Adriana Parrott, at Holy Trinity Church, Clapham, Surrey in 1847 and, by the time of the 1851 Census, they were living at 4, Marine Terrace with their two year-old daughter, Adriana Margaret Harris.

Meanwhile, 12-year-old William John Harris was at school in the City of London and boarding at 27 College Street in the parish of St. Michael Paternoster. He was entered on the medical register on October 8th 1859 and became a member of the Royal College of Surgeons that same year. In 1861, William John Harris was living with his father and stepmother at 4, Marine Terrace in Worthing and in practice as a surgeon and – like his father - general practitioner.

On May 24th 1866, he married Florentia Caroline Jeaffreson at Edmonton, All Saints, in Essex and they are shown living at 13, Marine Parade, Worthing for the 1871 Census. Their only child, Herbert George Harris, was baptised at Broadwater, on September 23rd 1874. William John Harris later moved to Church House in Lansdowne Road, Heene and appears to have retired from active practice around 1891 as a result of some form of paralysis.[29] Then, it was reported:[30]

> 'The victims of Typhoid unfortunately include a prominent and well-known townsman, Mr. William John Harris, who for many years was senior surgeon to the Worthing Infirmary. At one time Mr. Harris held the leading practice at Worthing and was universally recognised as a most skilful and able man. A year or two ago, however, owing to a distressing ailment, he was compelled to abandon his profession and retire into private life, followed by the good wishes of all who knew him. Mr. Harris was for many years Chairman of the Worthing Local Board, he was also Chairman of the Pier Company, and for two years in succession he was elected Deputy Master of the Worthing Lodge of Freemasons, to which he had been a subscribing member for many years. As Chairman of the Worthing Athletic Sports he took the greatest interest in promoting the success of its annual gathering. He was a member of the Meteorological Society, and his daily returns, made at the cost of much personal sacrifice and labour, were of the greatest value. Much sympathy is felt by all classes for Mrs. Harris and her son in their sad bereavement.'

William John Harris was buried in Heene Cemetery on August 28th. His estate amounted to £13,598. As for his father, William Harris, he was again widowed and, in 1891, living at Shelley House, Gratwicke Road with Minnie - a daughter from his second marriage who had married another medical man: Golding Bird Collet. When he died in 1896, he left some £23,989 in his will.

William Henry Kneller (By Mary Mckeown):

William was born in Kings Somborne, Hampshire on September 14th 1838 and his parents were Henry and Elizabeth, nee Freemantle. In 1851, William was living in Kings Somborne with his parents and his 2 siblings, Sarah and John. His father was working as an agricultural labourer, whilst William was recorded as a scholar. He must have excelled at his academic studies because – by 1859 – he had become the schoolmaster in the village of East Wellow.

The *Hampshire and Isle of Wight Directory* for 1859 describes 'East Wellow as a parish of scattered houses, adjourning that of West Wellow, in Wiltshire. It is about 3½ miles west south west of Romsey and contains 297 souls, and 2,810 acres of land, nearly all the property of Wm. Edward Nightingale Esq. of Embley House.'

Purchased in 1825, Embley House became the Nightingale family home as well as Lea Hurst in Derbyshire, which was their summer home. William Nightingale and his wife Frances were the parents of Florence Nightingale who is famously known as "The Lady with the Lamp". Mrs. Frances Nightingale supported the school in East Wellow, where William was the schoolmaster.[31] In 1861, William Kneller, now aged 22, was lodging with farmer, Charles Pope, and his family at Red Lodge, East Wellow.

▼ Dowse School, Broughton. William Kneller (standing right) was master here from 1874 to 1889 (BCA 44.01).

William married Anna Maria Bown on January 21st 1869 at All Saints Church, Charlton in the parish of Downton. They had 7 children but, sadly, three were to die in infancy. By 1871, William and Anna had made their home at 'The Grotto' in East Wellow. Then, three years later, William took up a new teaching position, which was reported in the *Hampshire Advertiser County Newspaper:*[32]

> 'SCHOOL APPOINTMENT – Mr. William Kneller, who for upwards of seventeen years has been the respected master of the National Schools, at East Wellow, near this town, and which are under the especial patronage of Miss Florence Nightingale and the family, has been unanimously chosen out of a large number of candidates by the trustees of the Broughton Endowed Boys' School to fill a similar post here. We congratulate Mr. Kneller upon gaining a more lucrative appointment, as well as the trustees in having a master so well suited for the situation.'

▼ Goring School, Mulberry Lane (JV).

He held the position of Master at Dowse School in Broughton from 1874 till 1889,[33] so in the 1881 Census, William and Anna are living at the Dowse School House in Broughton, Hampshire. They have two young children, Mabel aged 2 and baby William Freemantle aged 10 months. William's widowed mother Elizabeth was also living with the family. Another child, Edgar, was born later in 1881 followed by Henry in 1883.

By 1891, William had taken up a new position in Goring, Sussex. The family was now living at the school house in Goring, where William was the schoolmaster and Anna the schoolmistress but, by 1893, William had moved to West Tarring to start a new venture, which was advertised in the local newspaper:

> **'OPENING OF A MIDDLE-CLASS SCHOOL –**
>
> Mr. W. H. KNELLER gives notice that he will after Easter open a middle-class school for boys at West Tarring. MR. KNELLER, who has the highest references, is in a position to offer a good education upon moderate terms, and at his establishment boarders will find a comfortable home. Miss Kneller also will receive a limited number of younger boys and girls.'[34]

William established a small private school at 'Claydon,' South Street, West Tarring. The school would appear to be named after Claydon House in Buckinghamshire, where Florence Nightingale was a frequent visitor and it was also the home of her sister Frances Parthenope Verney. Sadly, William contracted typhoid fever later in the year, and after being ill for 35 days he died at 'Claydon' on September 3rd. He was 54 years old. William's brother, John, registered his death and he was buried in West Tarring Churchyard the next day.

His death was recorded in the local newspaper:

> '(he) was engaged for several years as Master of the Goring Parish Schools. He afterwards moved to Tarring where he established a small private school, but still continued to act as Assistant Overseer of the parish of Goring and Secretary of the Goring Benefit Society. He was an ardent cricketer and was secretary of the Goring Club. A genial companion, he will be greatly missed by the many friends he had made during his residence in the locality.'[35]

William was reported as having a long connection with Florence Nightingale. In an article in the *Worthing Gazette*, it was stated that his son, Henry, had recalled his father taking him to visit Florence in London. Henry explained that Miss Nightingale first took an interest in his father when he was a schoolteacher and had charge of the East Wellow, Hampshire, private school, with which the Nightingale family were associated. He also received his training as a teacher at the Queenswood College, in which they were also interested. Mr. Kneller, senior, spent a great deal of time with the Nightingale family when he was secretary to her for 16 years. He was with her parents when she was away in the Crimea War. He also helped to pack many of the bales of medical supplies Miss Nightingale urgently called for when she found the desperate need for them on the battlefield.

Various personal items were given to William from Florence, including a book *Early Years of the Prince Consort*, which was privately printed for Queen Victoria, with the inscription:

> 'William Henry Kneller, now 16 years Master of Wellow School. This record of a man who raised while yet in his youth, to share the throne of the greatest Empire on earth, appears to have thought of nothing but duty and self-sacrifice, and so continued till the last hour of his life acting up to his ideal is offered by his anxious friend. Florence Nightingale. London May 12th 1872.'[36]

Dr Ernest Cecil Haward Van Buren (By Colin Reid):

> 'Following closely upon the death of Mr W J Harris, we have
> with deep regret to record the decease of another medical man,
> Dr Van Buren having passed away shortly after noon today. Some
> six weeks since Dr Van Buren contracted typhoid, doubtless as
> a result of his close attendance of patients afflicted with that
> disease and, following the course of the fever, thrombosis set in,
> followed by the failure of the heart's action. Yesterday's bulletin
> declared that the patient was in a critical condition and the
> answer given to inquiries this morning that Dr Van Buren was
> surely sinking was supplemented later by the sad announcement
> that death had taken place'.[37]

While Dr Van Buren's maternal ancestry is plain, his paternal line is singularly confusing. It appears he was born illegitimately circa 1859 in the registration district of St George's, Hanover Square to Caroline Price. His mother was born at 12, Stafford Place, Pimlico on February 1st 1832 – a daughter of David Price (a tailor from the city of Gloucester) and his wife, Harriet (nee Biddell) from Holloway. The family were still living at that address at the time of the 1841 Census but, ten years later David and Harriet with their youngest child, Walter, had moved to 4, Cork Street. The whereabouts of Caroline are not known.

Although there is no evidence of Caroline marrying, we next find her at St Michael's Church, Highgate on June 10th 1860 for the baptism of her son, Ernest Cecil Alfred Haward. His father is given as James Hodges Haward, a distiller and their abode is in Hampstead. However, the announcement of Ernest's death[38] in the *Worthing Gazette* (presumably dictated by his mother) gives his father as James Cartwright Haward and in the same paper an article describes James Haward as a barrister-at-law. At the time of the 1861 Census, Caroline and Ernest are lodging at 17, Flask Walk, Hampstead. Caroline is now 27 years old and employed as a governess and she declares she is married but there is no sign of a husband.

Then, on November 25th 1865, Caroline married Martinus Robert Van Buren at St Mark's Church, Notting Hill. The witnesses at that ceremony were Caroline's brother and sister: David Biddell and Celia Price. Martinus was a 54-year-old merchant and a Freemason. When he was baptised at St Olave's Church, Hart Street, London on March 7th 1811, his date of birth was given as October 22nd 1810. Unless he was brought to England as a tiny baby, the assertion (presumably by his widow) in the *Worthing Gazette* for September 13th 1893 that he was from Rotterdam was incorrect. From the time of his mother's marriage, Ernest adopted his stepfather's surname.

Martinus died in 1868 and, on the 1881 Census, Caroline Van Buren was a matron in the Metropolitan District Asylum of Watford Union in Hertfordshire, together with her son Ernest who was a medical student. Ernest was placed on the *Medical Register* on 31 December 1881. By the time of the 1891 Census, Ernest was living with his mother at 9, Montague Place, Worthing and working as a general practitioner.

By 1893, Ernest's address was 'Ennismore', Rowlands Road and that is where he died on September 13th with his maternal aunt, Celia Price, present. The cause of death was given as enteric fever and thrombosis. He was buried in Heene Cemetery on September 15th, 1893, in the NW Section, row 2, graves 19 and 20. His mother, Caroline Van Buren, died in Worthing on 22 April 1907 and was buried with him.

There was a lengthy obituary published in the *Worthing Gazette* issued on September 13th 1893 and also the following shorter version extracted from the *Daily News:*[39]

'The death took place yesterday of Dr E. C. Howard Van Buren this being the second doctor who has succumbed to the epidemic. He has been ill for six weeks, having contracted the disease while in attendance upon patients at the temporary hospitals, and the fever was succeeded by thrombosis and failure of the heart's action. Dr Van Buren, who was only 34 years of age, was an M.R.C.S.Eng., L.R.C.P.Edin., L.R.C.P.London, and M.D. of Brussels, where he gained honours. He had held the posts of assistant house physician of St. George's Hospital, house surgeon of the Bucks General Infirmary, and house surgeon of Kensington Infirmary. He went to Worthing three years ago to take up a partnership with Mr. Simpson. In an interval between his occupancy of two of the posts named above, Dr Van Buren travelled all round the world with the Duke of Sutherland. He was an examiner of the St. John Ambulance Society and was author of 'A Book on Health in our Daily Lives'. He was unmarried'.

Among the large number of mourners was Miss McGavin whom Ernest was due to marry later in the year. Ernest had been a Freemason at the Worthing Lodge so, after others had quitted the burial ground his brother Masons dropped sprigs of acacia on his coffin.

By 1901, Caroline Van Buren was lodging at Edma House, Rowlands Road but when she died on April 22nd 1907 her domicile was 'Lucetta', Shakespeare Road. She was buried in the same grave space as her son.

Emily Gomes/Gomez – Known as Nurse Alice (By Mary Mckeown):

The following notice appeared in *The Portsmouth Evening News*:

'GOMES – On the 17th instant, at Whitcliff, St. James' Road, Hereford, of typhoid fever, contracted at Worthing, Emily Gomes ("Nurse Alice"), of Brompton Hospital, formerly of Gosport, aged 28.'[40]

Very little is known about Emily's early life or whom her parents were. It is also unknown why she chose to call herself Nurse Alice. According to the 1881 Census, she was born circa 1866 in Gosport, Hampshire; and she is boarding at Alver Cottage, Alver Road, Alverstoke. This is the home of Robert and Hannah Moorey and their two daughters Mary Annie, and Helen. Robert's occupation is a blacksmith at the dockyard, whilst his daughters are both recorded as governesses. There are two scholars living with them, one being, Emily Gomes aged 15.

By the time of the 1891 Census, Emily is now a governess, living with the Cooke family at The Gables, Alverstoke. Head of the household is George Cooke a master grocer who was born in Hereford, his wife Mary and 6 daughters who's ages range from 3 to 15 years. Then, in 1893, Emily is a hospital nurse in Worthing.

She contracted typhoid fever and had been ill for 8 weeks. Emily died on 17th November 1893 at St. James Street, Hereford. She was 28 years old. It would appear that Emily was held in high esteem by the Cooke family, as she died at the Cooke family home in Hereford. Edward Cooke of 6 Edinburgh Road, Portsmouth was present and registered her death.

A brass plaque in St. Botolph's Church, Heene is a permanent reminder of Emily (Nurse Alice) and the typhoid epidemic of 1893, it reads:

'TO THE GLORY OF GOD
AND IN LOVING MEMORY OF
NURSE ALICE
OF BROMPTON HOSPITAL, WHO DIED AT HEREFORD,
NOV 17TH 1893, OF TYPHOID FEVER
AFTER NURSING IN WORTHING AND HEENE
DURING THE EPIDEMIC OF THAT YEAR'

(MM)

Reverend Joseph Lancaster (By Colin Reid):

The Reverend Joseph Lancaster was a complex character – one it seems of independent mind who was prepared to speak out – but equally a dedicated vicar whose compassion for his parishioners led to his untimely death.

Joseph was born on September 5th 1844 in Church Street in the small Lancashire town of Padiham – the youngest of six children of Thomas by Ann Lancaster. When Thomas married Ann Diggle as a widower in Burnley on March 6th 1831, he was described as a labourer and they set up home with the two daughters from his first marriage: Elizabeth born in 1825 in Clayton-le-Moors (described as deaf and dumb in official records) and Mary born in Habergham Eaves in 1827. By 1851, as a family of eight, they were living in Gawthorpe Street, Padiham and Thomas was employed as a butcher. Ten years later, they were still living in the same house with Thomas Lancaster now described as a greengrocer and Joseph apprenticed as a joiner.

◀ Eliza Mary Pearson married Rev Joseph Lancaster on September 22nd 1880 in the parish church of Prestwich, Lancashire (MW).

By the time of the 1871 census, Joseph was now a qualified joiner and lodging at 3, Chatham Road, Hartlepool. From his obituary[41] in the *Worthing Gazette*, we glean that Joseph entered St Aidan's College in 1874 and was ordained as a deacon two years later. Midway through a curacy spanning 1876 to 1878 at St Luke's Church, Barton Hill, Bristol, he took priest's orders and afterwards was appointed vicar for Christ Church in Lowestoft. While there, on September 22nd 1880, he married Eliza Mary Pearson in the parish church of Prestwich back in Lancashire and, early in 1883, their son Victor Pearson was born.

After a five year tenure in Lowestoft, he was held in such high esteem that – before he left for Worthing – the churchwardens and sidesmen presented him with a portrait in oils of himself and they attached this message to the gold frame:[42]

> '(We) do hereby, on behalf of ourselves and the parishioners, beg yourself the acceptance of the accompanying portrait as a small token of our appreciation of the great kindness we at all times have received at your hands and of the valuable services you have rendered to us during your stay amongst us...'

So it was that – at the age of 39 years – Joseph Lancaster came to Worthing in September 1883 to become the first vicar of Holy Trinity Church in Shelley Road. This new parish had been carved out of the ecclesiastical district of Christ Church. With his wife and son, he moved into the Byron Road vicarage; and, from his detailed account, Elleray observed:[43]

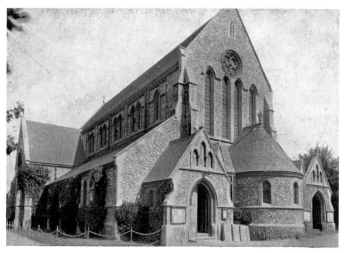

▶ On the left is Holy Trinity Church, Shelley Road where Joseph Lancaster was the first vicar and, on the right, is the High Anglican St Andrew's Church, Clifton Road. Rev Lancaster was immediately embroiled in a dispute over the existence of St Andrew's in his Parish (CR).

'A considerable measure of sympathy must be accorded to Joseph Lancaster in the St Andrew's affair, for immediately on arrival in his new parish of Holy Trinity he found himself embroiled in a quarrel in no way of his making in which he was forced to play a central rôle'.

Put simply, a group of local people (Wedds, Collets, Goldsmiths and several others) started meeting in 1881 as a movement outside the control of the Broadwater Parish Church to create a church of High Ritual within the bounds of Worthing; and they had the backing of the Bishop of Chichester, Richard Durnford, to further their aims but were opposed by the Rev Francis Cruse (vicar of Christ Church) and Rev Edward King Elliott (rector of St Mary's, Broadwater). Given the proposed new church of St Andrew's was within the newly formed parish of Holy Trinity, it was inevitable that Rev Lancaster would have to get involved in the debate but, being of an evangelical bent, he joined the opposition to St Andrew's enthusiastically. Indeed, with Rev Lancaster avowing his intention to legally contest the opening of St Andrew's, the consecration ceremony set by Bishop Durnford for November 30th 1886 had to be cancelled so close to that date that several hundred people arrived at the church oblivious that the event had been abandoned.[44] This was but a temporary stay – St Andrew's Church was eventually consecrated by Bishop Durnford on August 1st 1888.

The arrival of the Salvation Army with their militant evangelism in Worthing late in 1883, was met with incomprehension among the middle-classes and open hostility from some quarters of the working class. While some church leaders maintained a low profile during the disturbances, Chris Hare notes: 'On January 6th 1884, the vicar of Holy Trinity, the Rev J Lancaster, invited members of the Salvation Army to take the sacrament at his church. Fifty-nine Salvationists responded to this offer, and it appears that the service laid the ground for cordial relations'.[45]

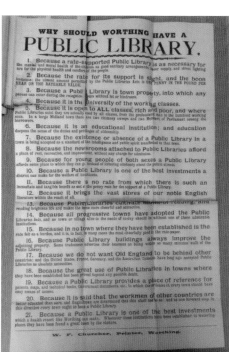

▶ Posters, measuring 2'6" x 1'5" appeared on hoardings across Worthing with 21 reasons why Worthing should have a public library (WMA).

From 1810, there had been a number of circulating libraries in Worthing, but by 1892 the town had still not adopted the Public Libraries Act of 1850. From 1890 onward, Robert W Charles (a young solicitor) spearheaded a campaign to open a public library in Worthing and in W F Churcher (a councillor and editor of the *Worthing Gazette*) he found an active ally. Large-scale notices appeared on hoardings all over the town publishing 21 reasons 'Why should Worthing have a Public Library.'[46] Rev Lancaster, in a particularly energetic anti-library campaign, financed a set of leaflets to be delivered to the doors of the poor throughout the town[47] – the rate-financed library, he claimed, 'will press heavily upon ladies and gentlemen with very limited means... a Public Library will be conducive to novel reading rather than healthy reading'. The matter was brought to a public meeting on November 30th 1892 – that and a ballot of ratepayers provided the go-ahead for a public library in Worthing.

Then, at the height of the second wave of typhoid fever, Rev Lancaster ruffled feathers when he wrote about Worthing Corporation in two local papers (including the *Sussex Coast Mercury*): 'Why don't they resign?' Two letters in the *Worthing Gazette*[48] – one anonymous and one from Alderman Melvill Green – rushed to the defence of the council but Green had to agree with the last sentence of Rev Lancaster's letter: 'At the least cost certainly, but at any cost however great, let us have without delay a supply of water sufficient to enable us to stop altogether supplying any houses for any purpose from the poisoned fount'.

From his obituary, we know that none of this activity detracted from his ministry. In his ten years as vicar of Holy Trinity Church: 'The debt upon the church was liquidated, a new Mission Room was opened, a new organ erected, the church enlarged, a spire with clock and bells built, a new vicarage provided and Schools for boys, girls and infants opened'. The same obituary relates: 'Apparently a strong-built man, Mr Lancaster was possessed of an indomitable energy, and that energy he unselfishly devoted to the duties pertaining to his holy calling; and whilst the minority of wealthy parishioners felt that in their pastor they had a man to whom they could look for instruction and guidance, the much larger proportion of poor parishioners recognised in Mr Lancaster a brother who never tired in his efforts to ameliorate their social and spiritual condition'.

There can be no better demonstration of that than his devotion to his parishioners during the typhoid epidemic. Members of the Typhoid Research Project have calculated he officiated at 39 funerals between May and October 1893 and - of these - 25 folks had died from typhoid fever. From September 6th through to December 5th, the curate at Holy Trinity Church (Rev E W Taylor-Jones) conducted a further five funerals that included two deaths from typhoid. Little wonder then that 'as a consequence of his unselfish and untiring exertions, he broke down and was ordered to Harrogate for a few weeks rest and change'. He resumed his visits to the sick and, with his wife, planned a few days at the home of his sister-in-law at Ingleside, Wimbledon Park in October – totally unaware that he had contracted typhoid himself. Great hopes were entertained for his recovery, but he died there on November 30th after 46 days of illness.

With Holy Trinity Church totally full and masses waiting outside, his curate (Rev E W Taylor-Jones) and the rector of Broadwater Church (Rev E K Elliott) conducted the funeral service on December 5th. Some 25 carriages were needed to convey 16 clergy and church officers preceding the hearse with chief mourners following. Several hundred persons on foot joined the procession that wended its way to Broadwater and Worthing Cemetery where a large number of people awaited its arrival – significantly including clergy from St Andrew's Church. The Reverends J Henderson, J O Parr and E K Elliott conducted a service of committal that fittingly concluded with those gathered singing: 'Now the labourer's task is o'er.'

Eliza never remarried and continued to live in Byron Road until her death on April 4th 1926. Five days later, after a funeral service at Holy Trinity Church, her body was interred in the same grave as her husband in Broadwater Cemetery.

1 Lidbetter, Mrs L K Letter, dated January 23rd 1977, preserved at West Sussex Record Office. MP 1390.
2 West Sussex Gazette, January 24th 1974
3 Worthing Gazette, July 19th 1893
4 Worthing Herald, April 15th 1938
5 Worthing Gazette April 2nd 1930
6 Sussex Daily News, April 17th 1938
7 West Sussex Gazette, January 24th 1974
8 GRO Marriage Certificate, Ref: Q1 1883, East Preston 2b 497
9 Sussex Daily News, op. cit.
10 GRO Marriage Certificate, Ref: Q4 1877, Alton 2c 329. They were married on December 30th 1877.
11 The War Cry, August 26th 1893
12 Littlehampton Gazette, March 14th 1924
13 WSRO: East Preston Union, Minute Books of the Board of Guardians, WG9/1/10 May 1892-Aug. 1894
14 Longley A, Alexandra Terrace, Worthing (1960), 12
15 This became Park Ward in 1902 when the borough was extended to include the major part of Broadwater and West Tarring.
16 GRO Marriage Certificate, Ref: Q2 1884, East Preston 2b 613. They were married on April 10th 1884.
17 Primitive Methodist Magazine (1903). Sketch of FC Linfield, Ex-Vice President of Conference, by Joseph Ritson.
18 GRO, Death certificate Ref: Q2 1896, East Preston 2b 203
19 Worthing Gazette, May 27th 1896
20 Worthing Gazette, August 5th 1896
21 GRO, Death certificate Ref: Q4 1896, East Preston 2b 225
22 Worthing Gazette, August 5th 1908
23 Worthing Gazette, December 14th 1910
24 Ancestry.com. England & Wales, National Probate Calendar (Index of Wills and Administrations), 1858–1966
25 Ibid
26 The Nursing Record Journal July 20th 1893
27 Foster, Joseph. Oxford Men 1880–1892 With a record of their Schools Honours and Degrees. Oxford, England: James Parker & Co., 1893.
28 The Daily Graphic for August 26th 1893
29 Worthing Intelligencer for September 2nd 1893
30 West Sussex Gazette for August 31st 1893
31 The Villages of East & West Wellow and the parish of St. Margaret of Antioch by The Hampshire Genealogical Society, Village Series No. 83.
32 The Hampshire Advertiser County Newspaper for March 7th 1874
33 The Village of Broughton and the parish of St Mary the Virgin by The Hampshire Genealogical Society, Village Series No. 35
34 Worthing Gazette of March 29th 1893
35 Worthing Gazette of September 6th 1893
36 Worthing Gazette of May 7th 1952
37 Worthing Gazette for September 13th 1893
38 Worthing Gazette for September 13th 1893
39 Daily News for September 14th 1893
40 Portsmouth Evening News for November 24th 1893
41 Worthing Gazette for December 6th 1893
42 Worthing Gazette for December 6th 1893
43 Elleray, D Robert, St Andrew's Church, Worthing – a History and Description. 1977
44 The West Sussex Journal for December 7th 1886
45 Hare, Chris. Worthing, A History. 2008
46 Charles, Robert W. 'Public Libraries' cuttings book preserved at Worthing Museum ref: 69/416 from February 1892.
47 Ibid. Two such leaflets: 'Some reasons why you ought to vote "NO" to the proposal for a Free Public Library'; and 'Why should Worthing have a Public Library' December 6th 1892 are contained in this book of cuttings.
48 Worthing Gazette for August 16th 1893

Chapter 4

Care & Treatment of Victims

By Colin Reid

COMMUNITY NURSING

Early in the epidemic, the Worthing District Nursing Association – at the request of Worthing Corporation – undertook the nursing of the sick at their own homes.[1] Extra nurses were engaged and – as their duties were arduous and the distances great – pony carriages were hired so that the sick might be visited at least once if not twice a day. Two Queen's nurses, the Misses Burkitt and Buckle, were associated with setting up the initial response to the epidemic – superintended by Miss Burkitt alone when Miss Buckle was afforded leave of absence. The nurses at their disposal were: Washington, Dawson and Wardrop (from St John's), Hutchinson and Gerrard (Devonshire House), Miss Costerton (from Holy Cross), and Miss Hopper and Sister Alice who had received specific training. When, toward the end of July, there were such large numbers to be treated the decision was made to find residences for these nurses scattered in different areas of Worthing. From August 14th, Miss Hopper superintended the stationing of a nurse in each of fourteen districts in the borough. This work was initially funded by the East Preston Board of Guardians and the Town Council.

HOSPITALS

Worthing Infirmary:

Following a public meeting chaired by the Rev Henry Dixon, a Dispensary was opened in Ann Street in 1829 'for the relief of the sick and necessitous poor of Worthing'. Dr J G Cloves (of whom more later) and consulting surgeon, Frederick Dixon, headed up the committee that gave oversight.[2] Through the generosity of Mrs Ann Thwaytes of Charmandean, a new building was erected in Chapel Road in 1846 and, with enlargement in 1860, became Worthing Infirmary and Dispensary.[3] With a rapid increase in the population of Worthing, it was deemed necessary to move the Infirmary to Lyndhurst Road but, initially, just two nine-bed wards (male and female) were built. A nine-bed children's ward was added in 1888. Within the Infirmary, on May 16th 1893,[4] Worthing Infirmary Committee made available nine beds to Worthing Corporation for typhoid patients, but the need was much greater.

▲ *Worthing Infirmary circa 1900, showing the lawn where two tents were erected to provide additional space for typhoid patients. Worthing Hospital in 2022 – the whole area to the south is now a car park (CR).*

Worthing Infirmary Tents:

On May 19th two 30ft by 16ft marquees were erected on the lawn in front of and to the south of the Infirmary.[5] Each catered for eight patients – one for men and one for women but, in the hot, dry weather that prevailed that year, conditions within these marquees became stifling despite aiding circulation by raising the sides and despite syringing the canvas rooves with water. The weather being so hot, the patients were practically lying in the open air all day. From research undertaken by Paul Holden, we know that 'a Mr H Feest recalled being treated in a tent on the front lawn of the Infirmary in 1893.'[6] Extra nurses were obtained under the supervision of the Infirmary matron. The tent for males was closed on July 11th and that for females on July 21st. Any remaining patients were moved into the Infirmary building.

FURTHER RESPONSE

At the same time, as the disease reappeared in July, it was clear that far more beds were needed and it was then that three temporary hospitals were opened for private and Corporation cases (Richmond House, Travellers' Rest and Mr Ralli's private hospital) and, for parish cases, the East Preston Guardians provided three more hospitals (Newland Road, Lyndhurst Road and High Street).[7] With the permission of Dr Kelly, a reporter from the *Worthing Gazette* visited all six of these during the morning of Sunday July 30th and his detailed account appeared in the following Wednesday's *Gazette* and informs much of the following.[8]

Richmond House:

Built circa 1837 as Chapel House to designs by Henry Cotton, for the residence of Dr Jeremiah Cloves, this was a substantial property on the northern corner of Chapel Road with Richmond Road, but it wasn't until 1880 that it took the name Richmond

▶ *Richmond House, Chapel Road circa 1900 looking south (AR); and Worthing Museum 2022 looking south (CR).*

House. Already in use as a convalescent home managed by Mrs St. A Horton, on July 7th 1893,[9] it was the first property to be offered to operate as a temporary hospital. The *Worthing Gazette* reporter, who visited this building opined: 'The house is both commodious and well-arranged furnishing ample accommodation for 40 patients and with extensive grounds to aid convalescence.' Until his election to the Town Council, Mr G B Collet had acted as medical superintendent – in early September, his brother Mr A H Collet took over that role. Other practitioners with patients at Richmond House were: Messrs F Parish, W S Simpson, P J le Riche and J D S Nodes with Drs Van Buren, Hinds, Fagg and Gostling.

The patients catered for in Richmond House fell into three classes: private patients, those whose fees were raised by friends, and club patients. At the beginning of August, there was a preponderance of adult females, but care was provided also for some men and a few children. The medical superintendent of Richmond House was supported by the patients' own medical practitioners, by voluntary practical help from Mrs Horton, her sub-matron (Miss Bottomley) and by the services of 13 nurses (Cavell, Maibin, Goodman, Magill, Bains, Marjorie, Caroline, Hughes, Waller, Johnson, Gladys, Gray and Ella). Richmond House had the addition of a mortuary.

◀ *Doctors, nurses and supporters outside Richmond House when it was being used as a temporary hospital in 1893 (WSP). Standing at the left of the picture are possibly Drs Parker and Opie. The gentleman standing at the back on the left of those wearing boaters is Councillor Frederick Linfield.*

At the initiative of the matron, some 40 or 50 who had been treated at Richmond House were invited back for tea and several hours of entertainment on the evening of February 1st the following year.[10] This suggests it had reverted to its former role as a convalescent home once the epidemic ended. However, in Worthing there had been a clamour for a public library and – for the period 1897 to 1906 – Richmond House acted as a temporary repository.[11] Meanwhile, in 1902, Marian Frost (appointed librarian in 1901) appealed successfully to the Scottish-born, American philanthropist, Andrew Carnegie, to fund a permanent home for the collection of books. The site was cleared in 1906 and the new complex of library and museum to designs by H A Crouch was opened in December 1908.[12] While the museum has continued in the northern half, the southern portion was vacated when the present library was opened in 1975; and – apart from temporary use as a Tourist Information Office – this part of the building has not been fully utilised.

Travellers' Rest:

The *West Sussex Journal*, in 1890, described the newly opened 'Travellers' Rest' as: 'A very fine building both inside and out.[13] It contains sleeping accommodation for 60 men, a good library well-stocked with books and newspapers and a capital kitchen.'

▶ *On the left: the Travellers' Rest in its early 1900s incarnation as St Edward's Hostel (AR). In the 1990s, the site between Clifton Road and Victoria Road was cleared for the building of Charles Court – pictured here in 2023 (CR).*

This substantial, 12-bedroomed property with a stable and coach house attached had a frontage of some 60 feet to the eastern side of Clifton Road. At the time of the 1891 Census, the lodging house manager was George Washington Munro who was resident with his wife, Lucy, and they had 34 men of working age boarding at that time with the addition of one four-year-old boy.

On July 17th 1893, the Travellers' Rest started receiving typhoid patients.[14] There was capacity for as many as 80 patients across eight wards on two floors. Dr Goldsmith as medical superintendent was supported by 'the kindly ministrations of the large staff of Nurses'. (Daytime: Rosamond, Marjorie, Jessica, Edith, Agatha, Sissy, Beatrice, Muriel, Kate and May. Night time: Stennie, Hettie, Lilian, Millicent, Emmie, Burroughs, Madge, Kate and Elise). All of these were under the superintendence of their 'courteous and agreeable' Matron Elma.) Visiting practitioners were: Messrs W S Simpson, A H Collet, E A Opie, G B Collet and P J le Riche with Drs Van Buren, Fagg, Gostling and Hinds.[15]

By the beginning of October, it was possible to cease its operation as a fever hospital – six mattresses were destroyed and the rest of the bedding disinfected. In April 1897, Messrs King & Chasemore put up this freehold property for auction,

◀ *Pictured outside the Travellers' Rest in 1893 left to right are: standing: Beatrice, Kate, Millicent, Dr Dickson, Dr Levick, Madge, Dr Hinds, Muriel, Cissy, Emmie, Stannie, Kate, Mr A Collet, Hetty, Lilian (in front of Hetty), Mr Bridgman, Marjorie, Mr Gardner (secretary) and Dr Gostling. Sitting on chairs: Dr Fagg, Mrs Goldsmith, Matron, Jessica, Mrs Cortis and Dr Goldsmith. Sitting on ground: May, Edith, Agatha, Elsie and Rosamund (WSP).*

emphasising its suitability as a restaurant or coffee house or conversion to a private residence,[16] but the belief is that it was purchased by the Salvation Army and renamed 'Fellowship House' for the training of overseas missionaries. Then, in the early 1900s, with a further name change to 'St Edward's Hostel', it operated as a rest home. Later still, it was put to use as a Labour Exchange. It was subsequently demolished and 'Charles Court' now occupies that plot.[17]

Mr Ralli's Private Hospital:

◀ Two views of the Terrace 95 to 83, Marine Parade, Worthing – an Edwardian view on the left and the same terrace in 2022 (CR). The house of Mr G A Ralli (number 87) is arrowed in both views.

This was situated at 'Bella Vista', 87, Marine Parade and, at the time of the 1891 Census, the Misses Ellen and Florence Heap were heading up a school there for some 12 boys. On July 26th 1893, 'Mr G A Ralli's munificent generosity enabled an appreciable addition to be made to the hospital accommodation.'[18] The two best rooms in the house with a sea view were set aside for the purposes of convalescence. The sister-in-charge was Miss McCarthy and the patients had the following nurses to assist: Axton, Pritchard, Cook and Worthington. The Doctors in attendance were: Messrs A H Collet, G B Collet, W S Simpson and E A Opie with Dr Van Buren. The first patient was admitted on July 25th. The *Gazette* reporter noted the following admonitory notice in the hallway: 'Visitors strictly forbidden to bring food etc into the hospital. All visitors breaking rules will not be admitted.'[19] This temporary hospital received 16 patients. It closed on October 17th.

St George's Mission Room, Newland Road:

◀ St George's Mission Room, Newland Road, Worthing. On the left circa 1905 (AR) and pictured in 2022 on the right (CR).

The current building in Newland Road was opened on Sunday July 1st 1883 to designs by George H Hewer, but it had its genesis back in the 1860s.[20] The mother church of St George's opened in 1868 on the corner of Church Walk and St George's Road but it remained largely isolated until the development of the surrounding area was completed in the twentieth century. Meanwhile, a Penny Theatre/Music Hall in Newland Road was being used for Sunday services but – as early as 1869 – Rev W S Lewis recognised it was inadequate to meet the needs from the great increase of

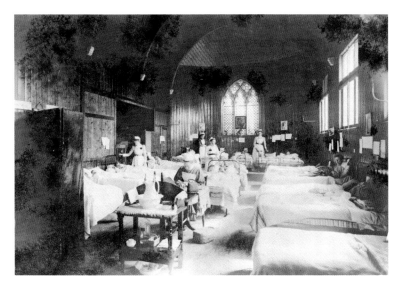

▲ Inside St George's Mission Hall, when it was being used as a temporary hospital in 1893 (WSP).

small tenements that were springing up in Newland Road – hence the campaign to make a new-build.

On July 12th 1893, it was the first temporary hospital to be opened for parish cases and, immediately, all 38 beds were taken.[21] The Committee of Guardians had appointed Mr E A Opie and Mr J D S Nodes (respectively assisted by Mr Henry Parker and Mr Nisbet) to superintend cases medically. There were two teams of nurses: Miss Freeman as nurse-in-charge daytime with Ross, Pracy, Hammond and Tranter, and Miss Stewart took charge of nurses Parker, Gardner and Driscoll at night time.

Sunday services continued in the Mission Room until it was redesignated the Foresters' Hall in 1936. Since then, it has variously been used as a school, a studio etc.

Iron Chapel, Lyndhurst Road:

This building has a most interesting history. The original siting was on the corner of Chapel Road and Wenban Road. The foundation stone was laid on September 24th 1879 and it opened as a chapel on January 4th the next year. Costing a little over

▶ Iron Chapel, Lyndhurst Road. On the left in 1898 (AR) and replaced by the Labour Hall in 2022 (CR).

£300, it accommodated 160 worshippers and was replaced by a brick-built chapel in 1892. Scarcely had it been re-erected in Lyndhurst Road as a Primitive Methodist Chapel in March 1893,[22] than it was used as a temporary hospital from July 15th,[23] providing beds for 21 patients in the chapel proper and a further 8 in an ante room. Miss Alice Courtney Clarke was the sister-in-charge assisted by the following nurses: Sweeting, Lawrence, Bellamy, Hodgeson, Mossman, Mason and Donnelly.

Following the epidemic, the Iron Chapel reverted to its intended purpose as a place of worship. Through the generosity of Mr J Hubbard, a new church was erected a little to the east of the Iron Chapel and opened for worship in October 1929. The Iron Chapel was sold to the Labour Party. In 1943, it was badly damaged by enemy action[24] and demolished after the War. The present Labour Hall was subsequently erected.

▶ Inside the Iron Chapel as a temporary hospital in 1893 (WSP).

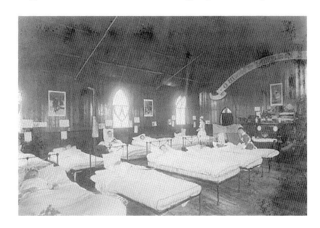

◀ The Hollies at 83, High Street, Worthing in 1954 (AR); and a remarkable survivor in 2022 (CR).

Girls' Training Centre, High Street:

This property, sited at the present day junction of High Street, Little High Street and Upper High Street, faces south at the northern end of High Street; and postally is deemed 83, High Street. This yellow brick villa was built circa 1810 to replace an existing building and was originally called North End Cottage.[25] For much of the 1800s, it was in private hands including a period in the 1820s when the Reverend William Davison lodged there. By the time of the 1891 Census, it was being run as a female servants' training centre with Catharine Cheeseman as superintendent, Mary Humphreys as matron and some 11 girls aged between 10 years and 18 years boarding and being trained there.

It opened as a temporary hospital on July 18th 1893[26] with 33 beds available but, given the small size of the rooms, this was across eight wards. The nurse-in-charge was Miss Crane who had the following nurses at her disposal daytime: Cooper, Hynes, Alloway and Faulkner, and night time: Lepelly, Redding, Pink, Newell and Banard. Under the supervision of Mrs Crowther-Beynon and supported by Fraulein Gregorson, cooked food was brought into the premises. For those patients who had recovered somewhat, a pleasant garden at the rear afforded opportunity for gentle exercise to aid convalescence.

◣ Doctors, nurses, other supporters and a few patients outside the Girls' Training School (The Hollies) when it was being used as a temporary hospital in 1893 (ML). The gentleman to the left of centre with his right hand on the back of a chair is Councillor Frederick Linfield and the gentleman toward the right of the picture with both hands on a chair is his brother, Arthur. Please note the man standing at the extreme right – he appears also in a photograph outside Richmond House. He has with him his trolley for moving dead people.

Broadwater Reading Room:

In April 1889, a Broadwater/Heene builder called Mr C Wright had his tender of £800 accepted for the building of a new Reading Room in Broadwater.[27] He worked

▶ On the left, Broadwater Reading Room when it was being used as a temporary hospital in 1893 (AR). Please note the gentleman on the left leaning on one of the temporary water tanks. On the right as Parish Rooms in 2022 (CR).

to designs by the architect, Robert S Hyde of Eriswell Road; and the building was opened that year in Broadwater Street West abutting two cottages to the east that had been constructed in 1884. The Broadwater Reading Room was comfortably furnished and supplied with the daily and weekly newspapers. There was a well assorted library and it was open Monday to Saturday from 8am to 10pm. It was paid for by public subscription and was administered by a management committee.

On July 20th 1893, it was converted to a hospital with two wards on the ground floor, capable of holding ten patients. It operated in this way till September 20th. In 1931, Miss Valetta Shout made these observations of 'those dark days' in Worthing:

> 'I was only 24 years old but I volunteered for service as a nurse. My district was Broadwater. I had the little Parish Room as a hospital and nursed patients on the floor there until beds could be procured. The work was strenuous, all the patients' milk having to be boiled and beef tea made at the Cricketers had to be fetched from there. I worked through all the trouble, then went to hospital to complete my training.'[28]

By 1898, it was being little used and, from 1900, the Parish Council took over its running as Parish Room and Reading Room.[29]

Old Palace, West Tarring:

▼ The Old Palace at West Tarring was being used as a school until it was requisitioned for use as a temporary hospital in 1893 (WSP). The photograph on the right shows how little has changed to this aspect of the Old Palace in 2023 (CR).

The Old Palace[30] in West Tarring is an extremely rare survivor from the medieval period in Worthing. It was the original manor house for West Tarring, comprising

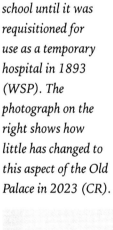

a hall with upper chambers of thirteenth century origin. It was remodelled in the fifteenth century with new window tracery and some reconstruction of the hall. The surviving building has been altered or restored on several occasions in the seventeenth, nineteenth and twentieth centuries. The rector, Jeremiah Milles, converted the building into a charity school in the mid-1700s and it remained as such (though not continuously) through to 1910.

The Infant Schoolroom was opened as a temporary hospital from August 9th till September 12th 1893 and some nine patients were admitted.

Reading Room, West Tarring:

On a cold day in February 1892, the Rev Dr W D Springett, visited the parish of West Tarring and saw that the Reading Room was nearing completion.[31] In

▲ West Tarring Reading Room has changed very little between its building and 2022 (CR).

May, he was inducted as rector and he was appointed a trustee in favour of his predecessor Rev Dr Henry Bailey. Dr Springett was instrumental in submitting for the approval rules and regulations for the future management of the rooms by a committee of members.

It was on April 15th 1891 that Mrs Emma Blake Clarke of Clarendon House gifted to trustees three cottages, so that the site at the corner of Glebe Road and South Street could be cleared and a Reading Room erected. On April 30th, the trustees were handed a cheque for £500. Five tenders for the building work were rejected in favour of one submitted by George Duffield which at £475 came in under budget. A loan of £100 was secured to pay for the furnishing of the property.

Under the Trust Deed, the primary object of this building was 'to be a Reading Room for the use, in their leisure hours, for men and youths occupied as artisans, mechanics, labourers or otherwise in agricultural trade in the village of West Tarring or its neighbourhood and likely to promote the intellectual, moral, social or material welfare and improvement of the working classes'.

The Reading Room was officially opened by the rector on July 27th 1892; and, at a meeting in the October, some 70 males of 16 years and over had enrolled as members at one penny a week to use both rooms – the one given over to the reading of newspapers and periodicals and the other to the playing of games such as cards, dominoes and draughts. Additionally, debates of national and local interest were organised every fortnight.

With cases of typhoid affecting West Tarring, all of these activities ceased so that the Reading Room could be converted to a temporary hospital on July 14th 1893. There was accommodation for 10 patients and some 23 local residents were treated there.

The Reading Room has continued to be governed by a Board of Trustees and let on a commercial basis with any surplus used for educational purposes.

CONVALESCENT HOMES

Marine Parade Convalescent Home:

This was situated at 95, Marine Parade.[32] At the time of the 1891 Census, it was operating as a lodging house. During the typhoid epidemic, it was made available as a convalescent home with a qualified nurse in charge under the superintendence of Mrs George Cortis. It received 127 patients.

▶ *The large three - storey building on the left of these pictures is 95, Marine Parade, which was made available as a convalescent home during the typhoid epidemic (CR).*

Goring Convalescent Home:

It was reported that Mr W F H Lyon 'made the Goring Home freely available as a Convalescent Home'. I take that to be Goring Hall or one of the cottages on that estate as, in 1891, William Francis Henry Lyon was living there with his parents, William (a JP and retired Army Major) and Louisa Lyon.[35]

▶ *Mr W F H Lyon made available 'the Goring home' as a place of convalescence. On the left as it looked before 1910 and, on the right, in 2023 (CR).*

A paternal uncle of W F H Lyon was David Lyon who had made a fortune as a merchant and slave owner out in the West Indies – specifically, Jamaica. In 1834, David Lyon purchased Northbrook Manor, later demolishing it and building Goring Hall in 1840.[33] Upon his death in 1872, the property came to his son, William. On Sunday August 5th 1888, there was a disastrous fire at Goring Hall that caused the destruction of the building. By virtue of his wealth, William Lyon senior was able to immediately rebuild the Hall in replica. He died in 1892 and William Francis Henry Lyon was the residual legatee of his father's will and – a year later – was in a position to make his Goring home available during the typhoid epidemic.[34] Some 54 patients recuperated there.

The Hall was leased to the Molson family from 1906 to 1933. At times during that period and afterward it was used as a school. In 1991, with the addition of a west wing it was set up as a private hospital – currently, Circle Health Group.

▼ *4, Victoria Terrace, South Farm Road was used as a convalescent home under the supervision of Rev Haynes, whose work was acclaimed (CR).*

4, Victoria Terrace, South Farm Road:

This was a recently built mid-terrace house on the eastern side of South Farm Road just south of the junction with Queen Street. It is now numbered 164, South Farm Road. In an October article in the *Worthing Gazette*, tribute is paid to Rev Charles Edward Haynes, curate at Broadwater, in this manner:[35]

'We the undersigned convalescents of Broadwater and West Tarring, desire your acceptance of this small token of respect and esteem which we have for your exceedingly great kindness to us during our stay at the Temporary Convalescent Home, 4, Victoria Terrace, Worthing. We know it has been at considerable personal inconvenience that you have ministered to our wants, and it will ever be our prayer that the blessing of Almighty God may rest upon you and yours'.

Upon its closure on October 3rd, Rev Haynes was presented with an illuminated address that listed the names of the 43 men and boys who had convalesced there. It appears he was assisted in that task by a staunch Methodist – Frederick Steele.[36] He had been a friend of the late Rev Joseph Lancaster and, at Easter 1894, he took over as minister at Holy Trinity Church.

John Horniman's House, Park Road:

From a trust established by the Quaker merchant, John Horniman, a Friends' Convalscent Home for Poor Children was opened at the southern end of Park Road in 1892 to designs by Brightwen Binyon.[37]

◀ The recently opened Friends' Convalescent Home for Poor Children (John Horniman) was used in that capacity during the typhoid epidemic. On the left in Edwardian times. Demolished in 2002, some 24 flats now stand on the site, 2022 (CR).

During the Worthing typhoid epidemic, some 54 children convalesced there.[38] It was the ex-mayoress (Mrs E C Patching) who had superintended their admissions there.

It was renamed the John Horniman Home in 1911 and then School in 1950 with particular emphasis on speech therapy. Despite vehement opposition from local residents and the Worthing Society, this very attractive building was demolished in 2002 to enable the building of 24 flats.

Poor Law Convalescent Homes:

In his report of 1894, Dr Kelly says: 'Poor Law Convalescent Homes were established for the reception of those who had been treated in hospital as Poor Law Patients.' They were under the immediate supervision of two of the guardians: Mrs Melvill Green and Mr Michael King.

◀ Midway along this row of houses on the eastern side of Eriswell Road is number 12 which was used as a Poor Law convalescent home for children (CR).

The photograph on the left is the original York Terrace – Chichester House is at the extreme right and was used for older Poor Law convalescents (QM). York Terrace was bought up by George Hilbery Warne, becoming the Warnes Hotel. During renovation the hotel was destroyed by fire. Fortunately, insurance covered the cost of the rebuild as on the right, 2023 (CR).

A letter in the *Worthing Gazette* identifies two such convalescent homes: beds for 10 children at 12, Eriswell Road – full since August 7th; beds for 30 older patients at Chichester House, York Terrace – full since August 23rd. There were three trained nurses in charge of these two homes.[39]

In his report, Thomson also refers to 'temporary accommodation at Milton House, Worthing'. I can find no other reference to this in any newspapers, reports etc and – for the time being – its location is uncertain as Worthing directories for this period list two properties called Milton House: one at 23, Milton Street and the other at 1, Warwick Place.

Convalescent Homes away from Worthing:

In his 1894 report, Dr Thomson makes reference as follows:

'Accommodation for convalescents from all invaded areas was provided in homes temporarily taken at... Findon...'

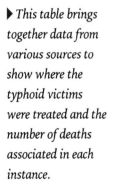

This table brings together data from various sources to show where the typhoid victims were treated and the number of deaths associated in each instance.

CATEGORY	NUMBER OF PEOPLE INVOLVED	NUMBER OF DEATHS
Patients Treated in their Worthing Home	931	111
Worthing Infirmary	27	10
Marquees in grounds of Infirmary	23	2
Richmond House	61	5
Travellers' Rest	91	20
Mr Ralli's Private Hospital	16	0
St George's Mission Room, Newland Road	70	17
Iron Chapel, Lyndhurst Road	55	7
Girls' Training Room, High Street	88	6
Broadwater Reading Room	22	3
Old Palace, West Tarring	9	3
Reading Room, West Tarring	23	2
Marine Parade Convalescent Home	127	1
Goring Convalescent Home	54	0
4, Victoria Terrace, South Farm Road	43+	0
John Horniman's House, Park Road	54	0
12, Eriswell Road	10+	0
Chichester House, York Terrace	30+	0
Out of Area Deaths	-	7

According to Green and Kelly, this commenced on June 14th.[40]

In their report, the Worthing Relief Fund Committee tendered particular thanks to:
'Mrs Wilson Saunders of the Saunders' Convalescent Home at Ramsgate through whose kindness several patients were received free of charge and to Mrs Grey of Bloomfield, Lindfield who made special arrangements for patients at her convalescent home'.

SOUP KITCHENS

Invalid Kitchen:

This opened on May 23rd and closed on June 24th – its whereabouts is not known.[41]

Relief Kitchen:

Poor's Relief Society began in 1870 and, in 1892, the Provident Relief Society built a soup kitchen to designs by A T Cooke in 'Dutch Renaissance style' on land controlled by the trustees of the Humphrey's Almshouses – currently 50, Grafton

◀ *The Provident Kitchen in Grafton Road is pictured in 2022 (MM). Every day for 24 weeks during the typhoid epidemic it produced large quantities of beef tea, jelly etc and the interior was captured on film in 1893 (WSP).*

Road.[42] On July 11th 1893, the committee of the Provident and Relief Society made available their relief kitchen 'for the distribution of necessaries to the sick'. It operated daily for 24 weeks and it was reported: 'The Provident and Relief Society's Soup Kitchen in Grafton Road is being utilised for the manufacture, upon a large scale, of beef tea, jelly etc.'[43]

The kitchen closed in 1922 and was sold in 1930. Thereafter, it was in commercial use (as example: Phillips & Dart, Electrical Engineers from 1934 to 1974+) until restored as 'Provident House' by Intelligence Business Services in 1992.

Ann Street:

Messrs Snewin owned properties at 33 and 35, Ann Street. They made one of those buildings available for running a temporary soup kitchen.[44]

Bath Place:

Lorenzo Ferrari opened a free soup kitchen in the old drill hall in Bath Place.[45]

◀ *In this 1920s photograph of the Theatre Royal, on the western side of Bath Place, the entrance to the drill hall can be seen to the far right. (AR)*

1 *Worthing Gazette for August 2nd 1893*

2 *Holden, Paul. 'Typhoid, Bombs and Matron – The History of Worthing Hospital'. 1992*

3 *Elleray, D Robert. 'A Millennium Encyclopaedia of Worthing History'. 1998*

4 *Kelly, Charles MD, FRCP 'The Epidemic of Enteric Fever in 1893 in the Borough of Worthing and in the villages of Broadwater & West Tarring'. 1894*

5 *Ibid*

6 *Holden, Paul. 'Typhoid, Bombs and Matron – the History of Worthing Hospital'. 1992*

7 *Ibid*

8 *Worthing Gazette for August 2nd 1893*

9 *Ibid*

10 *Worthing Gazette for February 7th 1894*

11 *Elleray, D Robert. 'A Millennium Encyclopaedia of Worthing History'. 1998*

12 *White, Sally. Worthing Past 2000*

13 *West Sussex Journal for August 19th 1890*

14 *Kelly, Charles MD, FRCP 'The Epidemic of Enteric Fever in 1893 in the Borough of Worthing and in the villages of Broadwater & West Tarring'. 1894*

15 *Worthing Gazette for August 2nd 1893*

16 *Worthing Gazette for April 28th 1897*

17 *Elleray, D Robert. 'A Millennium Encyclopaedia of Worthing History'. 1998*

18 *Worthing Gazette for August 2nd 1893*

19 *Worthing Gazette for August 2nd 1893*

20 *Kirshaw, G D S. 'St George's Parish Church'.*

21 *Kelly, Charles MD, FRCP 'The Epidemic of Enteric Fever in 1893 in the Borough of Worthing and in the villages of Broadwater & West Tarring'. 1894*

22 *West Sussex Journal for April 1th 1893*

23 *Kelly, Charles MD, FRCP 'The Epidemic of Enteric Fever in 1893 in the Borough of Worthing and in the villages of Broadwater & West Tarring'. 1894*

24 *Worthing Herald for July 2nd 1943*

25 *Elleray, D Robert. 'A Millennium Encyclopaedia of Worthing History'. 1998*

26 *Kelly, Charles MD, FRCP 'The Epidemic of Enteric Fever in 1893 in the Borough of Worthing and in the villages of Broadwater & West Tarring'. 1894*

27 *West Sussex Journal for April 9th 1889*

28 *Worthing Gazette for June 17th 1931*

29 *Kerridge, R G P and Standing, M R. Georgian and Victorian Broadwater 1983*

30 *Davies, Roger. 'Tarring – A Walk through its History'. 1990*

31 *Green, Chris. 'Revd. William Douglas Springett DD – Reading Room'. July 2007*

32 *Kelly, Charles MD, FRCP 'The Epidemic of Enteric Fever in 1893 in the Borough of Worthing and in the villages of Broadwater & West Tarring'. 1894*

33 *Fox-Wilson, Frank. 'The Story of Goring and Highdown'. 1987*

34 *Kelly, Charles MD, FRCP 'The Epidemic of Enteric Fever in 1893 in the Borough of Worthing and in the villages of Broadwater & West Tarring'. 1894*

35 *Worthing Gazette for October 4th 1893*

36 *Worthing Gazette for February 27th 1935*

37 *Elleray, D Robert. 'A Millennium Encyclopaedia of Worthing History'. 1998*

38 *Kelly, Charles MD, FRCP 'The Epidemic of Enteric Fever in 1893 in the Borough of Worthing and in the villages of Broadwater & West Tarring'. 1894*

39 *Worthing Gazette for September 13th 1893*

40 *Letter from Minnie Green and Charles Kelly in Worthing Gazette for August 9th 1893*

41 *Ibid*

42 *Elleray, D Robert. 'A Millennium Encyclopaedia of Worthing History'. 1998*

43 *Worthing Gazette for July 19th 1893*

44 *Letter from Minnie Green and Charles Kelly in Worthing Gazette for August 9th 1893*

45 *Worthing Herald for August 31st 1951*

Chapter 5
Relief Funds

Compiled by Malcolm Linfield

Introduction:

This chapter looks at two of the main relief funds set up to assist families suffering hardship because of the typhoid epidemic. By far the largest of these was the Mayor's Relief Fund, established by the Mayor of Worthing, Alderman Edward Patching in July 1893. The other fund was the inspiration of a local Wesleyan minister, the Rev. Thomas Evans, whose letter to the editor of the *Methodist Recorder* made a heartfelt appeal for financial support from the Methodist community. Although the scale of these relief funds was very different, both of them were very successful in their appeal for donations and significantly assist those individuals and families desperately in need of help.

HIS WORSHIP THE MAYOR OF WORTHING
(ALDERMAN EDWARD CUNNINGHAM PATCHING)

Initially it was thought that the epidemic would be of short duration and any distress could be met by 'local assistance'. In early June, Dr Charles Kelly, Worthing's medical officer of health and Mrs Melvill Green, one of the East Preston Guardians, took the lead when they voluntarily established a fund to alleviate the most urgent cases among the sick poor by providing 'necessary nourishment' during the progress of the illness and a change of air for convalescents in the countryside to speed recovery.[1]

◀Fig. 1: Portrait of the new mayor from the Worthing Gazette - 11 Nov 1891.

However, although well-intentioned, the fund 'was barely sufficient to do what was required',[2] and Councillor Captain Fraser proposed at a meeting of the Town Council on July 4th that the mayor be requested to invite subscriptions in the borough towards a fund for the benefit of the sick poor. After some discussion, Councillor Fraser's motion was unanimously carried. It was hoped that a town fund would be able to scale up to the challenges which the situation demanded, with the banks, libraries and the town offices ready to accept donations. By July 12th, £93- 16s-6d had been raised from the first contributions, mainly from members of the Town Council, various officials and other local worthies.[3]

THE MAYOR'S RELIEF FUND

By Malcolm Linfield

On July 15th 1893, a special committee – predominantly members of the Borough Council with representatives from the East Preston guardians and the church – was appointed to examine each application for assistance. The committee consisted of Alderman Patching (mayor), Alderman Piper (deputy mayor), Alderman Cortis, Councillors Butcher, Lea, Fraser, Smith and Linfield, the Rev. J.O. Parr, Mrs Goldsmith, Mrs Gresson, Mrs George Cortis and Mrs Melvill Green, with R. Grevett as hon. secretary. Each week, the local press published a list of subscriptions received, giving the names and the amount donated. On July 19th, the *Worthing Gazette* describes how the 'Mayor's Sick Fund' has 'met with very liberal support' and the 'energetic Committee' met every morning to examine the lists submitted by the clergy and 'medical men of the town' before sending out orders to local tradesmen for coal, milk and 'other necessaries'.[4] In all, they received many hundreds of applications, convening daily for several weeks; they also made a hard and fast rule not to give relief directly in money.

In the meantime, from July 11th, the soup kitchen in Grafton Road was placed unreservedly at the disposal of the committee by the Provident and Relief Society. Mrs Goldsmith and her admirable staff of volunteers were charged with making large quantities of beef tea, jelly and other nourishing foodstuffs, which would be distributed on a large scale daily with other medical necessities to the sick.

The deputy mayor, Alderman Robert Piper, had a letter published in the same edition in which he thanked subscribers for their generous support but stressed that because of the 'great amount of sickness' still prevailing, further funds would still be needed for the foreseeable future. He also appealed for blankets, sheets and linen which could be sent to the temporary hospitals. By July 26th, over 340 individual donations had been made with the amount received to date being about £550, including an anonymous subscription of £50.[5] On August 4th, the Sick Poor Fund managed by Minnie Green and Charles Kelly published a balance sheet, showing total receipts of £91-8s-11d, and how the money was spent on board and nursing for convalescent patients at Findon and elsewhere, plus the cost of 715lb of beef and mutton for making beef tea. The balance of £1-4s-2½d was passed to the Mayor's Relief Fund.[6]

The Worthing Relief Fund Committee published a report of their work up until April 21st 1894 in which they produced a balance sheet showing total receipts against total expenditure.[7] They also provided a list of the 'persons most particularly affected' by the epidemic, which, apart from the sick, included those people at serious risk of destitution because of the effect on their livelihoods, specifically amongst the 'Lodging-house Keepers, Boatmen, Bath-chairmen, Small Fly Proprietors, Small Traders, and Labourers.' The suspension of the tourist season and the collapse in a critical part of the local economy meant that many of them had no income at all to pay bills and buy the necessities of life. The committee 'strictly investigated' each application for assistance, taking great care to ensure that only those in genuine need received help. The ways in which the committee helped each of these groups is described in more detail later on, but fortunately, Worthing's substantial fruit growing industry seems to have escaped unscathed, as crops continued to be harvested and despatched by rail to the national markets throughout the epidemic.

By August 9th, a total of nearly £840 had been raised. However, weekly expenditure was currently exceeding £100, with 'immense quantities of milk' and £3 a day on brandy – 'given under medical instructions' – being sent out from the Provident Society's premises in Grafton Road. They were using 200lb of beef daily to make beef tea, and providing groceries and coal daily to nearly 200 families.[8] The milk was always scalded prior to distribution to ensure it was sterile and free of any possible contaminants. Such was the scale of the operation, involving the preparation of a hundred gallons of beef tea at any one time, that people were often required to work through the night.[9] The mayor organised a meeting of local tradesmen, which took place on August 15th at the Town Hall, to ask whether they could appeal to the their 'wholesale houses' on behalf of the Sick Poor Fund – a useful initiative which was to raise a total of £1,713-3s-10d (£181,000 today).[10]

Up to August 16th 1893, total donations had reached almost £1,200.[11] Although the local response had been incredible, it soon became evident that the crisis was going to need resourcing on a much grander scale and outside help would be required to meet the devastating impact of the disease. Lewes MP, Sir Henry Fletcher, who was also chairman of the East Preston Guardians, rose to the occasion and volunteered to send a letter to the London and provincial papers appealing for financial help, especially towards the cost of supporting typhoid patients in convalescent homes.[12] The response was immediate and money started to pour into the fund from all over the country, and especially from other towns in Sussex.

The Mayor of Brighton, Alderman Ewart, made an urgent appointment to see the mayor of Worthing to discuss the crisis in person, and after a long conversation, satisfied himself that the 'necessity for assistance was very great and very urgent'. He resolved to open his own Mayor's Relief Fund in Brighton, with subscriptions to be sent directly to the mayor or paid into the banks. As the money came in, they would send it on to the mayor of Worthing. The response was amazing, raising £774 (£82,000 today) in a week,[13] and was a great example to other Sussex towns who started to organise their own funds. Alderman Ewart attended a public meeting of the Hove Commissioners to give his support to the Chairman, Mr G B Woodruff, when he addressed the meeting at Hove Town Hall for the purpose of setting up its own committee to raise subscriptions. By the end of the meeting, a total of £153-1s-6d had been collected.[14] Other places soon followed, with promising subscription lists being started at Littlehampton, Lewes, Eastbourne, Hastings, Chichester, Arundel and elsewhere. By the end of August, funds received from all sources had leapt to about £3,750 (£400,000 today).[15]

Fund-Raising Endeavours:

Contributions to the Mayor's Fund came from every source imaginable. Countless village and church collections brought in significant sums, such as the generous £22-4s-0d collected in Hurstpierpoint by the Rector, Canon Borrer.[16] Businesses collected money from their employees, customers and suppliers, whilst many individuals collected money from their acquaintances, friends and relatives, all of whom received acknowledgment in the local press. In a number of cases, such as at Warren Farm and Southwick Manor Farm, employees forfeited their 'harvest home' celebrations to donate the cost to the Relief Fund. Mayors much further afield in the country also began to set up relief funds to help Worthing, including Tunbridge Wells in early September and Harrogate after the Rev. Joseph Lancaster, vicar of Holy Trinity, wrote a letter to the local paper whilst visiting the town.

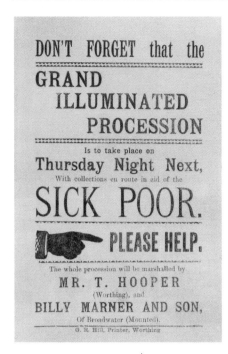

DON'T FORGET that the

GRAND
ILLUMINATED
PROCESSION

Is to take place on

Thursday Night Next,

With collections en route in aid of the

SICK POOR.

☛ **PLEASE HELP.**

The whole procession will be marshalled by

MR. T. HOOPER
(Worthing), and

BILLY MARNER AND SON,
Of Broadwater (Mounted).

G. R. Hill, Printer, Worthing

▲ *Worthing Bonfire Society organised an 'Illuminated Procession' on September 21st and raised £8-2s-11d for the 'Sick Poor' (WSP).*

Hundreds of special events were planned to raise money – their only limitation being the ingenuity of their organisers. Cricket benefit matches, cycling events, parades, recitals, street collections and smoking concerts made substantial sums, generously supported to help the people of Worthing in their hour of need. There are countless examples of different organisations doing their utmost to raise funds, one example being the Hove Friendly Societies who held a church parade in August which raised more than £55, whilst the *Sussex Daily News* Fund managed to raise over £225[17] before their fund was closed. Bonfire societies across the county held processions, taking their collection boxes with them. The mayor of Brighton set up a committee to organise a 'grand evening concert'[18] at the Dome on October 6th – which raised £117-13s-6d[19] – whilst Brighton Swimming Club gave an 'aquatic entertainment' at Brill's Baths, which was a game of water polo between Brighton and Bournemouth Swimming Clubs.

Donations in kind were also made, including bottles of port, brandy and whisky which were deemed important for their medicinal value, although unsurprisingly there was some controversy about their use, especially from within the Temperance movement who failed to see how alcohol could be anything but harmful, especially when given to children. But the use of alcohol as a 'stimulant' which could be used in 'extraordinary circumstances' was defended, as long as it was administered in prescribed doses like other medicine and the situation was serious enough to warrant it. Based on her own experience, Mrs G W Willett of Weston House, Brighton vigorously supported the use of alcohol in a letter to the *Sussex Daily News*, arguing that in cases of 'desperate illness when the exhausted life appears to hang upon a thread',[20] the use of an alcoholic stimulant saved lives. She was not advocating its use 'indiscriminately' but based on her experience in the treatment of more than 500 convalescents from the 'poorest classes' in London, where alcohol had been offered 'in cases of urgent necessity'.

In the meantime, more money was continuing to pour into the Mayor's Fund. In early September, a substantial sum was collected at Newmarket, where Mrs Dennis Thirlwell, with the help of Mr W C Manning, raised £100 from contributors who included 'many well-known trainers, racing officials, and jockeys'. At Covent Garden market, where much of the local fruit growers' produce was consigned, Mr George Monro successfully canvassed many of his contacts, collecting about £35-6s, which he sent to the mayor through Alderman Piper and Councillor Sams, both prominent local growers. Messrs Webber & Co raised a further £20-9s which reached the mayor through Barnwell & Magness, another local firm of fruit growers. By mid-September, the accumulated total of £5,500 had been raised for the fund, which included a generous sum of £170 raised in Littlehampton.[21]

During October 1893, some of the larger contributions came from other Mayors' Funds organised for the relief of Worthing. They included generous contributions of £109-10s-6d from Lewes, £150 from the people of Tunbridge Wells and £60 from Eastbourne.[22] At his last council meeting as mayor, on October 24th 1893, Alderman Patching announced that his fund had surpassed £7,000 and, on behalf of the inhabitants of Worthing, and as representative of the Town Council, he thanked all those who 'have so liberally contributed to, and otherwise assisted, the fund which has been raised to aid the sick, and those who have been and are suffering from the recent epidemic'.[23]

He singled out for special mention Sir Henry Fletcher, the editor of the *Sussex Daily News*; the mayors of Brighton, Lewes, Tunbridge Wells, Eastbourne and other towns; the chairman of the Hove Commissioners; the Relief Committee of Littlehampton; the Ladies of New Shoreham; the Friendly Societies of various towns and villages, and the churches; Mrs. Thirlwell; the tradesmen who appealed to the wholesale houses; the promoters and artistes of concerts and entertainments; the promoters of football, cricket, and stoolball; promoters of bicycle and other parades; the trustees of the Horniman Home; and the Freemasons, 'who were establishing a fund which was being collected in all parts of the world'.

Unsurprisingly, with the gradual abatement of the epidemic, subscriptions to the Mayor's Fund slowly declined. The amount collected in the week to 15 November was £132-2s-9d, which included a large subscription of £90, being the fourth and final instalment of the Hove Relief Fund.[24] The Borough of Worthing Bonfire Society, which held another illuminated parade on November 9th, contributed £2-11s-7d. By December 6th, gifts in kind included several bushels of apples, twelve rabbits – for one of the convalescent homes – and 103 new garments from Miss Johnson and her lady friends in Lancing.

Money was even being raised in India, where the Royal Sussex Regiment put on 'a variety entertainment' on behalf of the Worthing Relief Fund, which realised 200 rupees. A statement issued by the Winter Evenings Amusement Committee in December 1893, which was responsible for organising smoking concerts, showed accumulated profits of £5-14s-3d from three concerts.

Criticism of the Committee:

However, the committee of the Worthing Sick Fund was not without its critics. Local solicitor Henshall Fereday wrote a letter to the *Worthing Gazette*[25] in December 1893 complaining about the lack of transparency on how donations to the fund were being distributed. Part of his grievance, rather surprisingly, was that several of his friends were dismayed by 'local gossip' alleging they had been accepting relief from the fund. Fereday therefore criticised the committee for failing to produce balance sheets and asked that lists be published in the press each week to prove 'who have been recipients of relief' and remove any slanderous allegations against those accused of accepting relief. Fereday also contended that many property owners and landlords had benefitted 'rather more than the sick poor'.

Fereday's letter provoked a storm of criticism, not least because the committee had agreed right at the beginning that recipients of relief, through no fault of their own, should have their names protected from the stigma of pauperism which such lists might generate. Nevertheless, Fereday's attack may have inadvertently influenced the committee's decision to publish a report, which tries to fully elucidate their decision-making process.

Worthing Relief Fund – Committee's Report:

The Worthing Relief Fund Report was signed off by the Mayor, Robert Piper, on June 12th 1894 and published soon after. It endeavours to provide a detailed account of the groups of people whom the committee recognised as needing urgent assistance and how they devised what they regarded as the most effective way to achieve this targeted support.

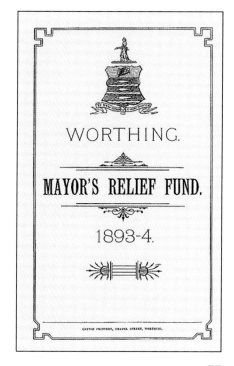

▼ *Fig 2.: Front page of the report of the Worthing Mayor's Relief Fund, 1894.*

The Sick: in the case of the sick, the issue of 'efficient Nursing' was the most urgent concern, so they subsidised the District Nursing Association, in partnership with the East Preston Guardians, to supplement their district nursing staff (£310-4s-1d). They also provided night nurses in several instances for those unable to afford it (£78-12s-5d).

The Lodging-house Keepers: caused the committee 'the greatest anxiety, for above all others they had lost every source of income, they had no means of paying rent, rates, and taxes, and in many cases no means of obtaining food'. Not wishing to be seen as diverting the fund into assisting landlords, they made a compromise whereby they would pay a sum of rent equal to that of the landlord as long as security of tenure was given until the summer of 1894, giving the tenant the chance of reviving their business. The committee spent £2,002-1s-4d, with the landlords contributing the same amount. In some cases, they also contributed food and fuel, and helped to prevent furniture being sold to pay rates and taxes to enable these businesses to open again when the time was right (£884-12s-6d).

Small Fly Proprietors: were seriously affected because their way of making a living had virtually ceased. The committee was able to assist their families and contribute towards the cost of keeping their horses through the winter (£19-0s-0d). **The boatmen, bath-chairmen, small traders and others** were mostly supported with food and fuel whereby they were provided with relief tickets. The total amount disbursed came to £1,084-18s, made up of meat, coal, groceries and bread.

The Labourers: The 'labouring class' was 'particularly affected' by being out of work due to the cessation of all building projects. The committee contributed £206-9s-10d to the Provident and Relief Society who were able to distribute coal once a week and soup and bread twice, but up to three times a week during the winter. In order to help families keep up with payments into their Friendly, Burial and Insurance Societies – since any reneging on contributions would sacrifice previous payments – the committee paid £40-2s. Families with serious and protracted illness were helped with medical costs, receiving between 30 and 50% according to circumstances (£497-5s-3d).

One of the major funding commitments was the relief kitchen in Grafton Road, and during the 24 weeks it was open, Mrs Goldsmith and her helpers were able to distribute to the sick a prodigious quantity of beef tea (1,629 gallons), milk (3,036 gallons), brandy (nearly 158 gallons!), custards (890), jellies (1,831), Valentine's Essence (963 bottles), eggs (7,679) and port wine (30 dozen) – at a total cost of £1,128-7s-5d.

The committee also provided grants to other people, as well as various organisations deemed worthy of extra support for the services they were offering. Although the committee had decided as a rule not to give relief directly in money, there was one exception made in the case of assisting domestic servants and others who had succumbed to the illness in Worthing and were recuperating with family in the country (£175-19s-4d). The committee also agreed to help families requiring financial assistance towards the cost of burial of a deceased relative, up to 50% (£38-10s). Other practical support was given to convalescents as it was in everyone's interests that they should recover quickly. A change of air was regarded as essential and arrangements were made with a number of places in the country to receive them, with the committee helping towards travel expenses and maintenance (£353-14s-7d).

Two convalescent homes were set up to expediate this process, one at Goring (Goring Hall) – the free use of which was provided by the owner – and one at 95, Marine Parade, Worthing. A qualified nurse was recruited to take charge of each, under the supervision of Mrs George Cortis. The cost of the Goring home came to £67-15s (for 54 patients) and Marine Parade £371-10s-10d (for 127 patients). Fifty-four convalescent children were given places at Horniman's Home in Park Road, generously offered to the committee by its trustees at a nominal charge of 2s-6d per head per week (£17-7s-6d).

Other local funds set up to help convalescents were given grants by the committee to support them with their work. One of these was established by two of the East Preston Guardians, Mrs Melvill Green and Mr Michael King, to take Poor Law patients ready to leave hospital, with all subscriptions acknowledged in the local press. They had a home for convalescing children at 12, Eriswell Road (with 10 beds) and another – for adults – at Chichester House, York Terrace (30 beds), with three trained nurses in charge of the two homes.[26] They were assisted with a grant of £180-0s-8d. Two other local funds raised in Broadwater and West Tarring to maintain convalescents, both received grants from the committee of £30 and £80 respectively. A number of patients, other than Poor Law patients, who were not able to afford their care were supported by the committee at the Retreat Hospital, in High Street (£68-1s-2d). Grants were also paid to the St. George's Poor Fund and the Worthing Needlework Society, which amounted to £35 between them.

The total amount raised by the Mayor's Relief Fund came to £8,803-4s-11d, of which £7,812.0s-6d had been spent at the time of the report. The balance in hand, some £991-4s-5d, was earmarked by the committee 'to form the nucleus of a Fund for the next winter'.

Controversy:

The committee continued to meet on a less regular basis, but controversy over the fund again erupted, this time from within, when one of its members, Councillor

Captain A B S Fraser, sent a letter to a number of papers in February 1895 announcing his sudden resignation from the committee with 'very strong protest' after discovering that ex-Councillor Tupper had been voted a sum of £25.[27] He claimed he didn't agree with the way money from the fund had been allocated and that it should go to the out-of-work men and their families in the town. Pursuing the same argument as Fereday in December 1893, he also thought that the recipients of relief should have their names published, against the principle adopted at the start of the fund that full disclosure of circumstances and relief granted would remain strictly private.

◀ Councillor Captain A B S Fraser – mayor of Worthing 1896/97 (CR).

Fraser was roundly condemned for his comments, not least by his fellow committee members, who couldn't understand why he had failed to raise his objections at any of their meetings. They also pointed out that he had only attended 14 of the 153 meetings, the last being on August 10th 1893, when the fund was only a month old, and that during the epidemic he deserted Worthing to go and live in Brighton. They failed to comprehend why he 'utterly failed as a member of the Committee in doing his duty... coming forward at this late hour to blame the members who remained in Worthing, and honestly, conscientiously, with painstaking care, and they believe successfully, discharged the important trust committed to them'. They also deeply regretted that the seal of confidence had been broken.

Known for his combative and petulant style, it soon became obvious that Fraser was only interested in pursuing his political ambitions in the forthcoming elections and it suited him to adopt a stand which distorted the truth and infuriated his former colleagues. Incidentally, on polling day, March 7th 1895,[28] Fraser lost the election in the north-west ward to the sitting incumbent Arthur Henty, who was duly elected county councillor, no doubt much to the relief of the many people he had offended.

It has not been possible to find out exactly when the Mayor's Relief Fund was wound up, but it would appear that by July 1895 there was only a small amount remaining. At the AGM of the Provident and Relief Society, the committee was gratefully thanked for a grant of £50, with the comment that since the fund was nearly expended, 'we cannot again look for the same help that we have received from it during the past two years'.[29]

THOMAS EVANS AND HIS EPIDEMIC RELIEF FUND 1893/94[A]
Researched by Marion Woolgar and edited by Malcolm Linfield

In August 2010, Marion Woolgar was doing some research at the West Sussex Record Office relating to non-conformist records for the Worthing area, when one of the archivists drew her attention to an item in the catalogue amongst the list of deposits from the Worthing Wesleyan Methodist Church. Intrigued, she requisitioned the item from the strong room and was fascinated with what she found, so much so that she couldn't put it down.

The document in question is a leather covered cash book measuring 6½ in by 4 in and bearing the title 'Epidemic Relief Fund 1893/94'.[30] Inside, the words *'AFFLICTED WORTHING'* have been cut from a publication and pasted on the reverse of the front cover. The first page of the book bears the title again, the total value of the fund and the signature of Thomas Evans, its treasurer. There then follows various letters to the editor of the *Methodist Recorder* and also a footnote from the editor commending the appeal to his readers, a list of donations and finally an auditor's certificate.

Reverend Thomas Evans:

Thomas Evans was born circa 1846 in Meifod, Montgomeryshire, the son of Richard and Sarah Evans. By 1861, he was an apprentice bookseller and stationer and living with his uncle, W. J. Thompson, in the Lime Street area of Liverpool. Then, at some time between 1861 and 1871, he enrolled as a student of theology at the Wesleyan College in Didsbury.

The Rev. Evans then embarked on a very busy period in his life. A directory of Wesleyan Methodist ministers and preachers published in 1896 lists his various appointments, including his periods of ministry at Bridlington and at Oakley Place Wesleyan Methodist Chapel in Peckham, SE London (Fig.3). In addition to his busy life as a Wesleyan Methodist preacher, the Rev. Evans's personal life took on a whole new dimension at this time. On August 27th, 1874, he married Ellen Hardy in the Wesleyan Methodist Chapel in Altrincham, Cheshire. Their first known child Thomas

[A] *We are grateful to the West Sussex Archives Society who have kindly granted permission to reproduce an edited version of Marion Woolgar's original article: 'Afflicted Worthing: Thomas Evans and his Epidemic Relief Fund 1893/94' for West Sussex Archives Society Journal No. 79 (2011) Page 3, ISSN 02645831.*

Howel Evans was born on June 21st 1875, also in Altrincham; and their son Oswald Hardey Evans was born on July 14th 1878 during his father's ministry in Chepstow, Monmouthshire. Sadly, just a few weeks before Rev. Evans was due to commence a new ministry in Witney, Oxfordshire, his wife died of rubeola (measles) on June 18th 1880 in Chepstow, aged just 31 years.

By the time of the 1881 Census, Thomas Evans was a widower and was enumerated in Ventnor on the Isle of Wight, a ministry that does not appear in his directory entry. Meanwhile his two sons Thomas (aged five) and Oswald (aged two) were living in the care of his sister, Mary Evans, in Hailey, Oxfordshire.

54	MINISTERS, ETC., IN GREAT BRITAIN		
1875 Liverpool, Shaw-street, do. 3	1890 Ferndale 2	1877 Wigton 1
1878 London, do. 8	1892 St. Keverne 3	1878 Cowbridge 2
1886 Bangor, do. 3	1895 Dunstable	1880 Banwell 2
1889 Llanrhaiadr, do. 1		1882 Banwell, Sup. 1
1890 London, Islington 3	EVANS, SAM. LEONARD.	1883 Bridport 1
1893 South Wales Mis., Welsh	Institution.	1884 Budleigh-Salterton, Sup. 3
	1894 Supply 2	1887 Redditch 3
EVANS, JOHN (c).	1896 Loftus-in-Cleveland	1890 Walsall, Centenary 3
1867 Cardiff, Welsh 2		1893 Alexandria 1
1869 Carmarthen, do. 3	EVANS, THOMAS.	1894 Hertford 2
1872 Aberayron, do. 1	1870 Institution 1	1896 Grays
1873 Brecon, do. 1	1871 Ross 2	
1874 St. David's, do. 2	1873 Truro 1	EVANS, WM. HUGH.
1876 Llanidloes, do. 1	1874 Cheltenham 3	1856 Amlwch, Welsh 2
1877 Treherbert, do. 1	1877 Chepstow 3	1858 Carnarvon. do. 2
1878 Ystumtuen, do. 2	1880 Witney 3	1860 Abergele, do. 1
1880 Brecon, do. 3	1883 Birmingham,	1861 Beaumaris, do. 2
1883 Carmarthen, do. 1	Newtown-row 3	1863 Llanfair, do. 2
1884 Lampeter, do. 3	1886 Bridlington 3	1865 Denbigh & Rhyl } 3
1887 Aberystwith, do. 1	1889 London, Oakley-pl. 3	1866 Rhyl, do. }
1888 Llanidloes, do. 3	1892 Worthing 2	1868 Llangollen, do. 3
1891 Llanfair, do. 2	1894 Highgate 3	1871 Dolgelly, do. 3
1893 Cefu, do. 3		1874 Mold, do. 3
1896 Llanfyllin, do.	EVANS, WESLEY J.	1877 Llanrwst, do. 3
	1877 Goginan, &c. 1	
	1878 Institution	
	1880 Institution	

▲ Fig 3.: Extract from a directory of Wesleyan Methodist ministers & preachers, 1896.

In 1883, Thomas Evans began a three-year ministry in Birmingham and he moved to Bridlington in 1886. In 1889, Thomas Evans began his ministry at Oakley Place

	£	s	d
½ x Quarters Stipend	18	15	0
Children	3	3	0
Carriage of luggage from London	3	17	6
Plus sundry expenses			

▼ Fig 4.: A letter to the editor of the Methodist Recorder in 1893.

Wesleyan Methodist Chapel in Peckham, SE London. The 1891 Census shows him reunited with his two sons and also with his sister, Mary, who was his housekeeper, and the family is living at 20 Trafalgar Road in Camberwell, in SE London. In this same year, the Worthing Wesleyan Society resolved to invite Thomas Evans to be their superintendent minister; and at the quarterly meeting held at Steyning on June 29th 1892,[31] it was reported that a letter had been received from the Rev. Evans accepting the invitation. Taking up his appointment on September 1st 1892, the circuit steward's account book[32] lists the Rev Evans' earnings for the quarter ending September 1892 as in the table above.

The following quarter, the Rev. Evans received his full stipend of £37-10s plus an allowance of three guineas for his children and his emoluments continued at that rate throughout his ministry in Worthing, although the extra payment for his children was reduced to £1-19s-6d as from the quarter ended June 1894, probably because his eldest child had reached a particular age. On March 29th 1893, Thomas Evans was invited to stay a second year at Worthing and within a few weeks, the first outbreak of enteric fever was reported in the town. Appalled at the effect that the disease was having upon the town of Worthing, Thomas Evans

WORTHING.

TO THE EDITOR OF THE METHODIST RECORDER.

DEAR SIR,—Will you allow me to bring before the attention of your readers the grievous calamity which has overtaken the town of Worthing—one of the pleasantest seaside resorts on the South coast—through a lamentable outbreak of typhoid fever. The epidemic broke out early in May, and, I am sorry to say, still continues, extending its ravages east and west. When it is stated that out of a population of 17,000 about 1,200 persons have been attacked, and of that number about one in ten have died, it will be seen that no more serious visitation has occurred to any community during the present generation. Whilst the epidemic has been no respecter of class or age, it has fallen most heavily upon the young and the poor, and the amount of suffering and distress entailed can hardly be exaggerated. The effect upon the town has also been disastrous, in the entire absence of visitors, the removal of many of the residents, the closing of schools, and the utter crippling of all trade and business. The outlook for all classes, and especially for the poor lodging-house keepers and tradespeople, is gloomy in the extreme.

But I desire especially to appeal on behalf of our own poor, many of whom are suffering grievously. The superintendent of one of our Sunday Schools, a bright and earnest young working man, has been taken, leaving a widow and child unprovided for (his youngest child died a few days before the father). Another young working man, a devoted member of our mission band, has also passed away, after a period of intense suffering, leaving a widow and six children to be cared for. About fifty of our Sunday-scholars have been among the sufferers, and seven have died. The period of convalescence for those who are likely to recover will necessarily be long, tedious, and costly. And there are many other sad cases.

The Mayor's Sick Fund, though generously supported, will by no means meet the whole necessities of the case. We therefore venture to appeal very earnestly on behalf of the members of our own branch of the Household of Faith in our greatly afflicted town at this time.

Contributions will be thankfully received by Mr. G. H. Lavender, 38, Montague Street, or by, dear Sir, yours faithfully, THOMAS EVANS, Wesleyan Minister.

34, Teville Road, Worthing.

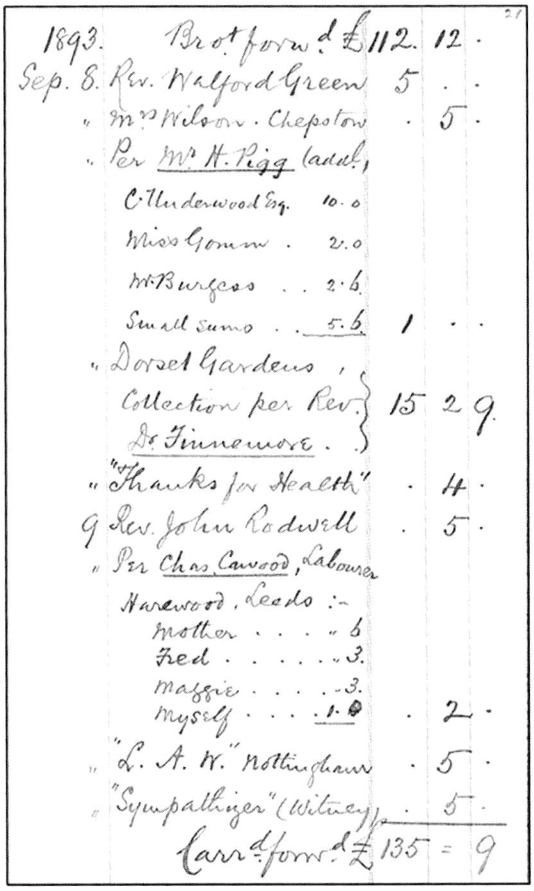

▶ Fig. 5.: A page from the Epidemic Relief Fund's Cash Book.

wrote to the editor of the *Methodist Recorder* making an impassioned plea on behalf of his congregation for financial assistance from the wider Methodist community. The full content of his letter appears opposite (Fig. 4):

The appeal fund started quietly. The first recorded donation arrived on August 24th 1893 with a donation of 7s-6d from the Rev J R Berry of Eastbourne, followed by three others the same day. Donations continued to arrive almost every day until October 13th after which the appeal started to ebb away until the fund was closed on March 17th 1894. Donations had arrived from all over Britain, including such diverse places as Bradford, Cheltenham, Glasgow, Lowestoft and St Austell; and also from Guernsey and Prince Edward Island in Canada. The

sums donated varied from ten pounds to a few pence, although there were also special collections at various meetings that raised larger sums. The congregations at Bridlington and Oakley Place, Peckham were particularly generous. The total donations amounted to £303-15s-9d plus 4s-2d in interest from the Post Office Savings Bank, giving a total fund value of £303-19s-11d.

There is an intriguing little mystery still to be solved. On the final page of the cash book is an entry recording that £242-0s-3d had been disbursed, presumably to the families of the victims of the epidemic and there is a footnote stating that the 'detailed list of disbursements is in the custody of Rev Thos. Evans', who by then was probably packing his belongings prior to his removal to Highgate. If that list of beneficiaries could be found, it would undoubtedly help to place on record the names of those who died of the epidemic. There was also a cash balance in the fund of £58-8s-7d on 24 August 1894, which doubtless the circuit stewards subsequently put to good use, although the balance is not shown in the circuit steward's account book nor in the circuit treasurer's cash book.[33]

At the Quarterly Meeting at Worthing on March 28th 1894, it was reported:

'That in retiring from the Superintendency of the Worthing Circuit, this Quarterly Meeting gratefully acknowledges the kindness and patience with which the Rev Thos. Evans has conducted the affairs of the Circuit during two years of particular difficulty and discouragement. It thankfully recognises his great regard and care for the poor especially at a time of very unusual and prolonged distress and affectionately sympathises with him and his beloved family in those circumstances which have made it incumbent upon him to ask for another appointment at the coming Conference.'

A Wesleyan Methodist ministry commences on September 1st and is usually for a three year period, subject to an annual invitation to remain. I have yet to discover what family circumstances prompted the Rev Evans to leave Worthing after just two years, but it is possible that his health may have suffered from the strain of coping with the typhoid epidemic.

Thomas Evans left the Worthing circuit on August 31st 1894 and the circuit steward's account book records that his final stipend for the September quarter was as follows:

	£	s	d
½ x Quarters Stipend	18	15	0
Charwoman at house		8	0
Travelling expenses to Highgate	1	10	0

After Highgate, Thomas Evans continued his ministry in Chertsey for three years, and then moved to New Barnet where he is recorded on the 1901 Census as living in Chipping Barnet, with his sister, Mary, and his son Oswald. His ministry at New Barnet was for three years and then he moved to Camborne, Cornwall.

On September 7th 1904 and during his ministry in Cornwall, Thomas Evans married for a second time. His bride was Susan Emily Hodgins and they married in the Wesleyan Methodist Chapel in Hinde Street, Manchester Square, St Marylebone, London. He retired from the active ministry in 1905 and settled in Barnet where he is shown with his wife on the 1911 Census, living with some of his wife's extended family.

Thomas Evans died on February 21st 1925 in Bournemouth. In his will, he left specific bequests to his two sons, Thomas Howel Evans of Argentina and Oswald Hardey Evans of Chile, and to his sister, Sarah Thomas. The residue of his estate was left to his wife, Susan Emily Evans.[34]

A short obituary to Thomas Evans was published in the *Minutes of the Wesleyan Methodist Conference* in 1925 and included the following words:

> 'As a preacher and pastor he won all hearts… He had
> a beautiful spirit, gentle as a child and loving to all. He
> was charitable in his judgement of others, generous in his
> appreciation of all efforts for good, fervent in his devotion to all
> the interests of the Kingdom of God.'

Thomas Evans's two year ministry in Worthing was certainly eventful. He was a man who both saw an emergency situation developing within his flock and also had the compassion to take practical steps to try and avert the worst of the consequences. His collection fund, raised as a result of just a single letter to the media, must have made a great deal of difference to his desperate congregation.

1 *Worthing Gazette, June 14th 1893*
2 *Worthing Gazette, July 5th 1893 p5*
3 *Worthing Gazette, July 12th 1893 p5*
4 *Worthing Gazette, July 19th 1893, p5*
5 *Worthing Gazette, July 26th 1893 p5*
6 *Worthing Gazette, August 9th 1893 p6 with corrected figures, Aug 16th 1893, p5*
7 *Worthing, Mayor's Relief Fund, 1893-4, Committee's Report, Caxton Printery, Chapel Street, Worthing, 1894*
8 *Worthing Gazette, August 9th 1893, p5*
9 *Worthing Gazette, July 26th 1893, p5*
10 *Worthing, Mayor's Relief Fund, 1893-4, Committee's Report p4, Caxton Printery, Chapel Street, Worthing, 1894*
11 *Worthing Gazette, August 23rd 1893, p5*
12 *Worthing Gazette, August 16th 1893, p5*
13 *Worthing Gazette, August 30th 1893, p6*
14 *Worthing Gazette, August 30th 1893 p6*

15 *Worthing Gazette, August 30th 1893 p4*

16 *Worthing Gazette, August 30th 1893 p5*

17 *Worthing Gazette, August 30th 1893 p6*

18 *Worthing Gazette, September 27th 1893 p5*

19 *Worthing Gazette, November 8th 1893 p5. Although the proceeds of the concert raised £117-13s-6d, after deducting expenses, the actual donation was £73-2s-10d.*

20 *Worthing Gazette, August 30th 1893, p6*

21 *Worthing Gazette, September 13th 1893 p5*

22 *Worthing Gazette, October 4th 1893 p5*

23 *Worthing Gazette, October 25th 1893 p6*

24 *Worthing Gazette, November 15th 1893 p4*

25 *Worthing Gazette, December 15th 1893 p5*

26 *Worthing Gazette, September 13th 1893 p5*

27 *Worthing Gazette, February 27th 1895 p5*

28 *Worthing Gazette, March 13th 1895 p6*

29 *Worthing Gazette, Jul 3rd 1895 p5*

30 *WSRO ref NC/M5W/2/1/6/1*

31 *WSRO ref NC/M5W/1/4/1*

32 *WSRO ref NC/M5W/1/8/1*

33 *WSRO ref NC/M5W/2/1/5/3*

34 *Proved June 26th 1925 Principal Registry.*

Chapter 6
Complete list of Typhoid Deaths

by Colin Reid

By an Act of Parliament that came into effect on August 3rd 1890, there was a requirement that any incidence of typhoid had to be notified to the medical officer – that is, Dr Kelly. In his 1894 report, Dr Kelly records there were five notifications to him of typhoid during the first quarter of 1893 – one in Worthing and four in West Tarring and, for those three months, there were two typhoid related deaths in Worthing and three in West Tarring. Here, we are concerned with deaths from typhoid in Worthing, Broadwater and West Tarring resulting from the contamination of the water supply after the April 14th incident. As Dr Thomson opines, these five deaths are anterior to the epidemic. During the course of our investigations, however, we have identified all five individuals that died from typhoid during the period January to March. They are:

- Arthur Edward Pomeroy, a 38-year-old inspector for Weights and Measures for West Sussex, became infected with typhoid at his Howard Terrace, West Street home and, a little more than a week later, he died in Worthing Infirmary on January 17th. Dr Simpson recorded the causes of death as: 'Typhoid Fever and Pneumonia'. At a Town Council meeting on September 5th, he was called to task because he had not notified Dr Kelly of that death at the time.[1][2]
- (Edith) Amy Smith was 11 years old and suffered with typhoid for 19 days before she died at home, 5, Normandy Terrace, West Tarring on January 18th.[3]
- Emma Jane Hart was 54 years old when she died at home (23, West Buildings) on February 21st. She had typhoid fever for 20 days.[4]
- Mabel Alice Henson* was 8 years old when she died at home, 3, Gordon Terrace, West Tarring, on March 13th having suffered the effects of typhoid for 90 days.[5]
- Edith Abram Henson* – a six year old sister of Mabel, died at home on March 19th, after 46 days with typhoid.[6]

The log book for Heene School notes the Henson sisters lived in a house where the drainage was not perfect.

In the table that follows are listed all 194 known deaths from the typhoid epidemic in Worthing in 1893. It is in alphabetical order according to the surname given on the death certificate. In the column for Burial Date & Place, the dates are coloured according to the following key to reveal the burial place:

■ Broadwater Cemetery

■ St Andrew's Church, West Tarring

■ Heene Cemetery

■ St Mary's Church, Goring

■ St Mary's Church, Washington

■ Out of County

NAME ON DEATH CERTIFICATE	DATE OF DEATH ON CERTIFICATE	PLACE OF DEATH	BURIAL DATE & PLACE – see key above	OCCUPATION	AGE ON DEATH CERT.
Alabaster, Henry William West	July 13th	6, York Road	July 17th	Retired Master Baker	65
Alderton, John	August 2nd	Training Home, High Street	August 4th	Hawker	28
Alford, Edmund John	May 29th	8, Buckingham Road	June 2nd	Journeyman Baker	23
Allen, Lilian Florence Adeline	August 10th	Travellers' Rest	August 12th	Domestic Parlour Maid	19
Allen, Richard James Cobden	August 7th	Travellers' Rest	August 9th	Draper's Porter	21
Allen, William John	May 22nd	Laundry, Richmond Road	May 24th	General Dealer	21
Andrews, Harry James Middleton	September 4th	2, Becket Road	September 6th		11
Apted, Ivy	August 6th	Broadwater	August 9th		9 months
Arnold, Sarah	August 6th	Villa St Albans	August 8th		57
Ayling, Alfred	July 11th	61, Clifton Road	July 14th		12
Baber, Sarah	July 19th	St George's Mission Room	July 21st		47
Bacon, Javen James	July 26th	Travellers' Rest	July 27th	General Labourer	18
Baker, Annie	July 9th	47, Clifton Road	July 12th	Laundress	19
Baker, William George	June 12th	17, West Street	June 14th	Journeyman Bricklayer	24
Beach, Harry	August 17th	Mission Room, Newland Road	August 19th	Milk Carrier	17
Beach, Kate	August 14th	3, Brunswick Road, Heene	August 15th		9
Beach, Sarah Ann	July 19th	Ivy Cottage, Broadwater	July 20th		29
Belton, Elizabeth Emily Kate	August 31st	15, Chapel Street	September 2nd		13
Bishop, Helena	November 30th	3, Church Cottages	December 2nd		76
Blunden, Edwin	July 25th	St George's Mission Room	July 27th	Bricklayer's Labourer	31
Braby, Ernest Edward	July 23rd	Iron Chapel, Lyndhurst Road	July 24th	Journeyman Painter	19

NAME ON DEATH CERTIFICATE	DATE OF DEATH ON CERTIFICATE	PLACE OF DEATH	BURIAL DATE & PLACE – see key above	OCCUPATION	AGE ON DEATH CERT.
Brazier, Eveline Florence	June 8th	Clifton Arms	June 12th		10
Bricknell, Kate	July 30th	High Street Hospital	July 31st		14
Bridger, Adeline Mary Tremearne	May 29th	4, Bath Place	June 2nd		14
Bridger, Edward	May 23rd	51, Clifton Road	May 27th		4
Bridges, Margaret Ellen	August 13th	Travellers' Rest	August 15th	Domestic Kitchen Maid	15
Broadbridge, Ellen	August 15th	Washington	August 16th		14
Burrell, Caroline	August 9th	Lillieshall, Lyndhurst Road	August 12th	Laundry Maid	21
Burtenshaw, Kate	July 26th	4, James Cottages, Heene	July 28th	General Domestic Servant	19
Butcher, Rose	August 23rd	Travellers' Rest	August 25th	General Domestic Servant	16
Butcher, Sarah	July 7th	1, Bartlets Cottages, Broadwater	July 8th		45
Caplen, Annie	May 16th	12, London Street	May 20th		42
Carter, Ann	July 11th	Richmond House	July 12th		69
Chandler, Sarah Ann	May 28th	91, Newland Road	June 1st		31
Chaplin, Gordon	June 5th	Surrey County School, Cranleigh	June 7th		15
Chapman, Mary Ann	August 16th	St George's Mission Room	August 18th		37
Charles, Emily	July 23rd	St George's Mission Room	July 25th		38
Charles, George	June 11th	118, Station Road	June 13th	Market Garden Labourer	18
Chipper, Annie Louisa	August 20th	Northbrook Cottages, Broadwater	August 21st	Domestic Housemaid	18
Churcher, Charlotte Mary	July 21st	35, Chapel Road	July 22nd		4
Churcher, Harriet	July 3rd	35, Chapel Road	July 7th		39
Clifford, Annie Gertrude	August 15th	21, Lennox Road	August 17th		12
Collings, Ella Louisa	June 7th	Elladale, Tarring Road	June 10th		6
Collins, William Charles	June 29th	Worthing Infirmary	July 4th	Journeyman Painter	32
Comper, Lizzie	July 18th	3, Howard Street	July 21st		10
Compton, Mary	August 23rd	Training Home	August 25th		27
Cook, Evelyn Eliza	May 29th	40, Park Road	May 31st		13
Coppard, Isabella	October 22nd	95, Marine Parade	October 25th		40
Covey, Emily	August 6th	West View, Heene Road	August 8th	Domestic Housemaid	18
Davidson, John Angus	June 5th	28, Lennox Road	June 7th	Tailor's Apprentice	18
Dawson, Octavius Gerald	August 10th	5, Palmerston Terrace	August 12th, St Nicholas' Church, Tooting	Independent Means	25
Dear, Charles Albert Holcomb	September 24th	Mission Room, Lyndhurst Road	September 26th		8

NAME ON DEATH CERTIFICATE	DATE OF DEATH ON CERTIFICATE	PLACE OF DEATH	BURIAL DATE & PLACE – see key above	OCCUPATION	AGE ON DEATH CERT.
Denyer, Sarah	August 20th	Travellers' Rest	August 22nd	General Domestic Servant	21
Dorey, Eliza	July 15th	3, Bartletts Cottages, Broadwater	July 15th		29
Duffield, Abraham	May 27th	Worthing Infirmary	May 30th	Market Garden Manager	34
Duffield, Frank	July 20th	West Tarring Reading Room	July 21st	General Labourer	27
Duke, James	August 9th	Travellers' Rest	August 11th	General Labourer	26
Duncan, Winifred Vassie	September 4th	Seaforth, Heene	September 6th (or 5th)		4 months
Dunn, Catherine Lavinia Eliza	August 17th	Coastguard Station	August 18th		7
Eade, Stephen	June 4th	16, Gloucester Place	June 7th	Fisherman	35
Elder, Arthur	May 18th	Lyndhurst Road	May 20th	Gasfitter at Gas Works	29
Eldridge, Violet Annie Kate	July 22nd	28, South Street	July 24th		18
Ellis, Sarah	July 21st	'Kingsclere', Worthing	July 25th, Norwood Cemetery	School Proprietress	59
Everest, Annie	July 25th	St George's Mission Room	July 28th	Hawker	32
Eyre, George Henry	July 29th	24, Orme Road	July 31st	Journeyman Compositor	26
Farrant, Francis Westhall	July 10th	'Belmont', Tennyson Road	July 14th, Great Malvern	School Master	27
Ferguson, Sophia Frances	August 22nd	5, Milton Street	August 23rd	Formerly a Governess	62
Field, Mary	August 8th	Mission Room, Newland Road	August 10th		50
Fifield, Frederick Walter	June 7th	Gasworks Cottage, Park Road	June 9th	Fruitgrower's Assistant	19
Fisher, Sarah Frances	July 16th	24, South Street	July 19th		54
Gomes, Emily	November 17th	St James' Street, Hereford	?	Hospital Nurse	28
Goodman, George Charles	July 23rd	Travellers' Rest	July 25th		17
Gordon, Elizabeth Caroline	July 20th	9, London Street	July 24th		23
Graham, Lottie	July 16th	Worthing Infirmary	July 19th	Domestic Housemaid	17
Gravett, John Dunford	June 10th	26, West Street	June 13th	General Labourer	20
Guiel, Arthur Edward	September 7th	Crunden Cottage, Newland Road	September 9th		22 months
Habgood, Charles Seymour	June 16th	22, Montague Street	June 17th	Draper's Apprentice	15
Harris, William John	August 28th	Church House, Heene	August 28th	Surgeon	55
Hartfield, Edward	August 12th	St George's Mission Room	August 15th	General Labourer	39
Hatcher, Percy Lionel	July 15th	7, St George's Terrace	July 18th		6

NAME ON DEATH CERTIFICATE	DATE OF DEATH ON CERTIFICATE	PLACE OF DEATH	BURIAL DATE & PLACE – see key above	OCCUPATION	AGE ON DEATH CERT.
Hawksworth, Edith Emily Maria	July 5th	Worthing Infirmary	July 7th	Sick Nurse	34
Hearsey, Mary	July 8th	35, Market Street	July 11th		51
Hedger, Ada Emily	July 15th	Richmond House	July 19th		13
Henson, David	August 13th	West Tarring Reading Room	August 14th	Agricultural Labourer	36
Herbert, Edith Sarah	July 24th	Sunnyside, Broadwater	July 26th		15
Hills, Fanny Esther	August 19th	6, Heene Cottages, Heene	August 19th	Dressmaker	18
Hills, James	August 15th	1, Chapel Street	August 16th	Corporation Employee	50
Hillyer, Hilda	June 7th	1, London Street	June 10th	General Domestic Servant	19
Hillyer, Mabel Gertrude	June 10th	57, Orme Road	June 14th		13
Hoare, Edith	August 4th	St George's Mission Room	August 5th		19
Holland, Charles James	August 1st	61, Newland Road	August 3rd		4
Hubbard, John George	August 26th	Mission Room, Lyndhurst Road	August 28th	Market Garden Labourer	20
Hughes, Emily	August 29th	St George's Mission Room	August 31st	Domestic Housemaid	17
Humphrey, Alice	May 26th	Sugden Road	May 27th	General Domestic Servant	15
Jackson, Ethel Mary	August 27th	Rutland House, Gratwicke Road	August 29th		16
Jarchow, Hermann Christian Francis	September 10th	Merstham, Surrey	September 14th St Katherine's Church, Merstham		12
Jeffries, Sydney Herbert	July 17th	8, Lyndhurst Road	July 19th		12
Johnson, Edith Emily	August 18th	Broadwater Reading Room	August 19th	Domestic Housemaid	17
Jordan, Alice	May 28th	17, Liverpool Gardens	June 1st		34
Joyes, Thomas	July 22nd	Travellers' Rest	July 24th	Bricklayer's Labourer	22
Keeble, Susan	August 17th	Temporary Hospital, Newland Road	August 19th		65
Kettle, Harold James	July 30th	17, Warwick Street	August 1st		14
Kimpton, Elizabeth	July 22nd	Travellers' Rest	July 24th		11
Kneller, William Henry	September 3rd	'Claydon House', Tarring	September 4th	School Proprietor	54
Laishley, Emma Maria	August 12th	Temporary Hospital, West Tarring	August 14th		32
Laishley, Ethel Eliza	August 16th	Iron Chapel, Lyndhurst Road	August 17th		7
Laishley, Frederick	August 20th	Iron Chapel, Lyndhurst Road	August 21st		9
Laker, Walter Frederick	August 20th	Ham Arch	August 22nd		2
Lancaster, Joseph	November 30th	Ingleside, Victoria Road, Wandsworth	December 5th	Clerk in Holy Orders	49
Lawman, Edith	July 30th	17, Marine Place	August 1st		12

NAME ON DEATH CERTIFICATE	DATE OF DEATH ON CERTIFICATE	PLACE OF DEATH	BURIAL DATE & PLACE – see key above	OCCUPATION	AGE ON DEATH CERT.
Leach, Jean	October 6th	Temporary Hospital, Lyndhurst Road	October 9th		42
Lelliott, Ann	July 15th	15, Market Street	July 18th		47
Lelliott, Annie	July 27th	Worthing Infirmary	July 29th		15
Lelliott, Mary Adelaide	July 13th	14, Zion Terrace	July 15th	Laundress	23
Lindup, Henry	August 4th	Travellers' Rest	August 7th	Journeyman Carpenter	28
Lloyd, Ethel	June 18th	Worthing Infirmary	June 20th	General Domestic Servant	16
Lovegrove, John Augustine	July 18th	62, Grafton Road	July 20th		23
Madgwick, Edgar Tom	June 9th	22, Market Street	June 12th		7
Marley, Esther	August 11th	Richmond House	August 12th	Dressmaker	21
Marner, Amelia Kate	July 19th	29, Clifton Road	July 22nd		6
Mears, Margaret Elizabeth	July 26th	Travellers' Rest	July 28th	General Domestic Servant	19
Millson, Mary Ann	July 27th	Travellers' Rest	July 29th	General Domestic Servant	26
Mitchell, Bertie Norman Clare	June 9th	Worthing Infirmary	June 13th		13
Morgan, William	July 8th	15, Lennox Road	July 11th	Independent Means	68
Murphy, John Wilfrid	August 16th	Coastguard Station	August 18th		6
Murrell, Mary Louisa	August 2nd	St George's Mission Room	August 4th		28
Muzzell, Alice Jane	November 1st	17, Ham Arch	November 3rd		29
Muzzell, Caroline	August 21st	Mission Room, Lyndhurst Road	August 23rd		6
Muzzell, George	August 30th	Mission Room, Lyndhurst Road	September 1st		5
Naldrett, Caroline Ellen	July 9th	6, Warman Terrace	July 11th		37
Newington, Guy	July 21st	3, Warwick Street	July 24th		12
Old, Mary Gouger	May 17th	10, Chapel Road	May 19th		35
Olding, Emma	August 18th	Travellers' Rest	August 19th	Laundry Maid	19
Olliver, Elizabeth	July 22nd	St George's Mission Room	July 24th		32
Osmand, Frederick	August 12th	Training Home, High Street	August 15th	Brickmaker's Labourer	18
Overington, Ellen	August 7th	Travellers' Rest	August 10th	Laundress	30
Pacy, Mary Isabel	June 11th	15, New Street	June 15th		11
Page, Annie Edith	September 18th	13, Ham Arch	September 21st		9 months
Page, Harriet	September 26th	Temporary Hospital, Lyndhurst Road	September 29th		32
Parks, Walter Thomas	July 22nd	Worthing Infirmary	July 25th	Domestic Gardener	18
Patching, Ambrose	August 16th	43, London Street	August 18th	General Labourer	30
Pearson, Lilian	May 23rd	School House, Newland Road	May 25th	General Domestic Servant	25

NAME ON DEATH CERTIFICATE	DATE OF DEATH ON CERTIFICATE	PLACE OF DEATH	BURIAL DATE & PLACE – *see key above*	OCCUPATION	AGE ON DEATH CERT.
Phillips, Ann	July 29th	20, Howard Street	July 31st		41
Piercy, Alfred Ambrose	July 16th	Steyne View, York Road	Smethwick Old Church		9
Pitney, Louisa	July 17th	59, Newland Road	July 20th	Dressmaker	24
Poore, Frederick William	August 9th	St George's Mission Room	August 11th		8
Potter, Lewis	July 12th	8, Bedford Row	July 15th	Retired Master Grocer	70
Ralfe, Alice Jane	May 22nd	1, Clifton Road	May 25th		31
Reeves, Emily Florence Lowder	August 17th	47, Sinclair Road, Hammersmith	?		12
Reynolds, Elizabeth Ellen	May 21st	11, Hertford Road	May 25th	Dressmaker	19
Rich, William	November 24th	88, Montague Street	November 27th	Master Paperhanger	47
Richards, Miriam	May 19th	6, Western Place	May 23rd		20
Riddles, Ellen	October 4th	Temporary Hospital, High Street	October 6th	Domestic Cook	37
Riddles, Ellen May	August 18th	13, Becket Road	August 19th		5
Riddles, James	August 22nd	Heene Road	August 23rd		12
Riddles, Martin	September 13th	Temporary Hospital, Tarring	September 14th	General Labourer	35
Rowley, Harry	August 22nd	7, Chapel Street	August 24th	Domestic Coachman	58
Sanders, Emily	July 20th	Richmond House	July 24th	Domestic Housemaid	21
Sayers, Percy William	May 25th	35, Cobden Road	May 30th	Master Watchmaker	25
Scrase, Annie	August 12th	St George's Mission Room	August 14th		33
Scutt, Rose Harriet	August 12th	Temporary Hospital, Tarring	August 12th	Domestic Housemaid	17
Searle, Edith Elizabeth	August 22nd	Lyndhurst Road	August 24th		16
Sheppard, Arthur James	May 22nd	27, Paragon Street	May 25th	Journeyman Carpenter	21
Shires, Annie	May 24th	12, Stanley Road	May 27th		12
Short, Deborah	August 21st	Broadwater Reading Room	August 22nd		36
Silvester, Henry	August 19th	2, Eastern Villas, Broadwater	August 19th	Retired Police Superintendent	60
Simson, John Miles	July 14th	'Turnhill', Bexley Road, Eltham	July 17th St John the Baptist Church, Eltham	Civil Engineer	22
Slaughter, Albert	July 19th	43, Market Street	July 22nd	Jobbing Gardener	20
Smith, Louise	May 27th	'Remenham', Victoria Road	May 30th		19
Sparkes, Washington	August 9th	5, Newcastle Terrace	August 11th	Jobbing Gardener	27
Stace, William Edward	July 29th	Broadwater Reading Room	July 29th	Journeyman Blacksmith	36
Stafford, Thomas Henry	May 20th	13, Cobden Road	May 24th	Fruit Grower's Labourer	18
Standing, Edith	August 8th	33, Market Street	August 11th		4
Standing, Mark	August 17th	Travellers' Rest	August 19th	Domestic Coachman	24
Standing, Sidney	May 22nd	22, Howard Street	May 26th		5

NAME ON DEATH CERTIFICATE	DATE OF DEATH ON CERTIFICATE	PLACE OF DEATH	BURIAL DATE & PLACE – *see key above*	OCCUPATION	AGE ON DEATH CERT.
Stevens, Lilian Caroline	June 7th	20, Park Road	June 10th		25
Street, Ellen Mary	July 9th	12, King Street	July 11th	General Domestic Servant	23
Stringer, Albert	June 18th	Worthing Infirmary	June 21st	Domestic Coachman	24
Strudwick, Ernest Pilch	May 25th	34, Stanhope Road	May 27th	Journeyman Painter	20
Taulbut, May	July 21st	St George's Mission Room	July 24th		11
Tickner, Alice Carrie	December 13th	27, Marine Place	December 15th	General Domestic Servant	15
Tier, George	June 21st	17, Station Road	June 24th		2
Till, Sarah Jane	August 24th	St George's Mission Room	August 26th		24
Town, Annie Ellen	July 23rd	Travellers' Rest	July 25th		27
Treagus, Caroline	July 28th	Training Home, High Street	July 31st		26
Tupper, Harry	August 26th	123, Newland Road	August 28th		6
Van Buren, Ernest Cecil Haward	September 13th	'Ennismore', Rowlands Road	September 15th	Surgeon	34
Ware, Lily	August 4th	Travellers' Rest	August 7th	Laundress	19
Warren, Ruth	November 21st	28, Richmond Road	November 23rd		8
Webb, Francis Llewellyn	August 22nd	Travellers' Rest	August 25th		7
Whittington, Mary	May 26th	73, Clifton Road	May 29th		73
Williams, Benjamin	July 28th	Richmond House	July 29th	Market Garden Labourer	24
Wingfield, Clara Emma Jane	August 7th	Travellers' Rest	August 9th		10
Wood, Florence Bessie	May 18th	Worthing Infirmary	May 22nd		12

All of the information is drawn from the individual death certificates, save for the burial details. The column for occupation has been left blank for children and for women whose rank is defined by their husband's occupation.

1 *Worthing Gazette for September 6th 1893*

2 Thomson, Dr Theodore. '*Report to the Local Government Board on an Epidemic of Enteric Fever in the Borough of Worthing and in the Villages of Broadwater and West Tarring*'. *1894*

3 Huxley-Williams, Muriel G. '*A brief story of Heene in the County of Sussex*'. *1973*

4 Thomson, Dr Theodore. '*Report to the Local Government Board on an Epidemic of Enteric Fever in the Borough of Worthing and in the Villages of Broadwater and West Tarring*'. *1894*

5 Huxley-Williams, Muriel G. '*A brief story of Heene in the County of Sussex*'. *1973*

6 *Ibid.*

Chapter 7
Facts and Figures – an Analysis

By Caroline Nelson, BA (Hons) Hist (Open)

Introduction:

Except for a few obituaries and funeral reports, little was recorded about the individual victims of the typhoid epidemic and the two official reports written by Dr Charles Kelly and Dr Theodore Thomson did not list their names. There were conflicting statements in the contemporary newspapers with the *London Evening Standard* claiming that a 'considerable number of the well-to-do class have been attacked and the proportion of deaths have been greater amongst them than the poor',[1] whereas the *Pall Mall Gazette* declared that the poorer classes had been most affected.[2] By identifying every victim, the Typhoid Research Project has allowed their individual stories to be told. However, creating a database using the information given on each death certificate, as well as the figures provided by Kelly and Thomson in their reports, enables the people who died to be analysed as a group. This chapter presents various statistics about the victims including which class, gender, and roads were most affected, and determines whether the *London Evening Standard* or the *Pall Mall Gazette* was correct.

Worthing's Health Reputation:

In 1890, Worthing and West Worthing (Heene Parish) had been incorporated as the Municipal Borough of Worthing. However, even though the epidemic was labelled 'Worthing' it also affected West Tarring and Broadwater villages. In 1893, the total estimated population of Worthing borough and the two villages was 19,290[3] so the typhoid epidemic's death toll of 194 was extremely high, particularly when compared to the Spanish Flu Pandemic in 1918 which killed 62 people[4] from a population of approximately 33,000.[5] Worthing's seaside economy relied not only on its year-round mild climate but also on the fact it was beneficial for people's health. The council publicised the town using its low mortality figures and in 1850, they had declared 'there is only one town in the kingdom where fewer deaths occur in proportion to the number of inhabitants.'[6] This claim can be substantiated by the *Worthing Sanitary Report* of 1893 which shows that the mortality rate for Worthing borough in 1892 was 14.4 per 1,000 persons living compared to 19.0 per 1,000 persons living in England and Wales.[7]

▶ *Fig. 1: Number of burials for Broadwater & Worthing Cemetery (BWC), Heene Burial Ground (St Michael's Road), Broadwater, West Tarring and Christ Church Churchyards 1849-1900.*

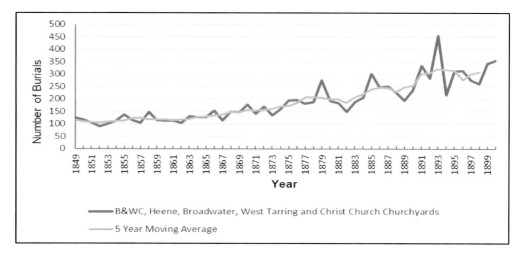

In 1893, the main burial ground was Broadwater and Worthing Cemetery which was opened in 1863 because space in the local churchyards, particularly St Mary's in Broadwater, started to reach capacity. However, the burial ground at Heene and the churchyards at St Andrew's in West Tarring and Christ Church in Worthing were also used to bury people who had died in those respective parishes. An analysis of the number of burials in Broadwater and Worthing Cemetery, and Broadwater, Heene, West Tarring, and Christ Church churchyards[8] shows a pronounced spike in the number of burials in 1893 which indicates a mortality crisis; that is, a sudden increase in the death rate (Fig. 1). The death rate for this year in Worthing borough was 24.5 per 1,000 persons living due to the excessive number of deaths from typhoid.[9]

Number of Typhoid Cases:

The typhoid epidemic lasted from April to December 1893 with a lull from June 10th for three weeks; so, the epidemic attacked in two waves with the second being far more deadly. However, while the outbreak in Worthing and Broadwater was at its height in July, West Worthing and West Tarring's outbreak peaked in August – see Table 1.

▶ *Table 1: Number of typhoid cases showing dates of attack for each month in each area which illustrates the peaks in the different areas.[10] Attack was defined by Kelly on page 8 of his report as the day the person called the doctor, could not work, or went to bed ill.*

Month	Worthing	Broadwater	West Worthing (Heene)	West Tarring	Total
April	9	1	0	0	10
May	259	2	0	1	262
June	176	5	2	3	186
July	560	22	8	9	599
August	169	7	35	34	245
September	63	0	9	3	75
October	15	3	1	5	24
November & December	10	2	3	0	15
Total	**1261**	**42**	**58**	**55**	**1416**

Final Death Toll:

The Typhoid Research Project has concluded that the final named death toll was 194. However, this does not appear to tally with the two official reports written individually by Thomson and Kelly who themselves reported different totals; Thomson recorded 186[11] and Kelly recorded 188.[12] However, both authors did not include the seven people who caught typhoid in Worthing, but whose deaths were recorded elsewhere; including John Simson, a civil engineer who died in Eltham, and Gordon Chaplin, a 15-year-old schoolboy who died at Surrey County School in Cranleigh after returning there for the summer term. Thomson only reported the figures up to the end of November, thus missing the death of the final victim, Alice Tickner, who died on December 13th. Kelly did not publish his report until June 1894 so included the final victim in his total. However, Kelly recorded one extra female death in Worthing; this is either an error in Kelly's count or the Typhoid Research Project has missed a death (although every death certificate for the Worthing area registered between April to December 1893 in the East Preston registration district has been checked), or Kelly may have included Emily Gomes, a nurse and an out-of-area death, in his total; as she may have become ill in Worthing and been notified as a typhoid case to him before travelling to Hereford for treatment.

Thomson	Kelly	Typhoid Research Project
186 (to the end of November)	**188** (includes Alice Tickner death in December and Emily Gomes, out-of-area death)	**187** Worthing registered deaths
1 December death missing (Alice Tickner)		
7 out-of-area deaths	**6** out-of-area deaths	**7** out-of-area deaths
194	**195**	**194**

◀ *Table 2: Chart demonstrating the typhoid death totals for Thomson, Kelly and the Typhoid Research Project.[13]*

Cause and Progression of Typhoid/Enteric Fever:

Typhoid, otherwise known as enteric fever, is caused by the bacteria *Salmonella Typhi* and is transmitted by consuming water or food contaminated with the faeces of an infected person.[14] The historian Jacob Steele-Williams argues that in the 1870s, typhoid was considered by most public health authorities as the 'pre-eminent filth disease'.[15] In 1893, the only treatment was supportive care. The illness lasted three to four weeks with the victim first suffering headaches, insomnia and feverishness. Their temperature would gradually increase, and diarrhoea and a rose-spot rash would often be present. These symptoms would intensify for a few weeks, then the patient would recover or die from exhaustion, bowel perforation, internal haemorrhage, or pneumonia.[16] The progression of the disease can be seen from the cause of death on the death certificates; for example, Annie Chipper, an 18-year-old domestic housemaid, fought typhoid for 50 days before dying of exhaustion; and Stephen Eade, a 35-year-old fisherman, died 40 hours after his bowel perforated having suffered typhoid for 28 days. A total of 52 victims have it reported on their death certificates that they suffered typhoid for 21-28 days before dying. However, the degree of information regarding the cause of death varied according to the doctor signing the certificate. In total, 22 doctors signed death certificates for the people who died in Worthing and the other three areas, including Ernest Van Buren, a 34-year-old surgeon who himself died of typhoid on September 13th. Edward Opie, a medical practitioner aged 33, worked all through the epidemic and attended the most deaths signing 37 certificates, followed by surgeon John Nodes, aged 24 years, who signed 24 certificates, and surgeon Augustus Collet, aged 49 years, who signed 18.

Total Mortality Rate:

Dr Kelly stated in his report there had been 1,416 cases of typhoid in Worthing, West Worthing (Heene), Broadwater, and West Tarring.[17] Using this figure, the typhoid mortality rate for this epidemic was 13.2% which corresponds with the expected typhoid mortality rate, when it is untreated, of 10 – 20%.[18]

There were also typhoid cases and deaths caused by the Worthing epidemic in the surrounding Sussex parishes. Kelly's *1893 Annual Report of the Condition of the Combined Sanitary District of West Sussex* describes how there were scattered cases of typhoid at Lyminster, Angmering, Warningcamp, Salvington, Tortington, Goring and Burpham, nearly all of which were imported into those parishes from Worthing. He also found that:

- In Steyning Sanitary District there were ten cases originating from female servants who had been sent back to their homes or from men who worked in Worthing and had drunk the polluted water, and another two cases due to infections passed to members of these households; one of these deaths may have been a 16-year-old domestic servant named Harriet Stringer who died from typhoid on July 30th 1893.
- In Westbourne Sanitary District there were three cases of enteric fever from Worthing from which two victims died. It is probable that they were:
  - Gertrude Mary Knight, aged 16 years, from East Ashling, who died on July 22nd 1893 and
  - Elizabeth Emma Harfield, aged 20 years, from West Ashling, who died on July 28th 1893.

▶ Table 3: Number of typhoid cases and deaths (Worthing and non-Worthing) for the surrounding rural and urban sanitary districts, and number of cases caused by the Worthing Typhoid Epidemic. Horsham U.S.D. did not operate the Infectious Disease (Notification) Act so the total figure is unknown for this area.[19]

	Total Cases	Total Deaths	Cases caused by Worthing Typhoid Infection
Steyning R.S.D	27	6	12
Horsham R.S.D	11	1	0
Petworth R.S.D	12	1	0
Thakeham R.S.D	17	4	9
East Preston R.S.D (does not include West Tarring or Broadwater)	22	4	22 approximately
Midhurst R.S.D	13	1	3
Westbourne R.S.D	10	2	7
Littlehampton U.S.D.	13	1	8 approximately
Arundel U.S.D.	16	2	1
Horsham U.S.D.	3	3	0
Total	**144**	**25**	**62 approximately**

Another four members of these infected households also caught typhoid.

- In Thakeham Sanitary District, seven cases of enteric fever were bought to the area by girls in service who had been sent home when the first symptoms of illness appeared; it is highly likely that one of these girls was Caroline Annie Vaughan, aged 19 years, who died on August 13th 1893 at her newly-married sister's home in Washington. Caroline is shown on the 1891 census working as a domestic servant at 91 Marine Parade, Worthing. A further two residents of these infected households in this District also caught typhoid.
- Littlehampton had approximately eight cases from Worthing.
- Arundel had one; she recovered.
- Midhurst had thirteen; three of whom were servants who were sent home and developed the disease after their arrival.

In total, there were 144 typhoid cases for 1893 notified in Worthing's surrounding parishes, of which approximately 62 were infections caused by the Worthing typhoid epidemic. There were two deaths in Westbourne directly attributable to the epidemic. Kelly did not state how many of the deaths in the other districts were caused by the epidemic but, using the 13.2% mortality rate, it is likely to be approximately seven.

A precise final figure of cases and deaths caused by the Worthing typhoid epidemic will probably never be known as typhoid has an average incubation period of one to two weeks, but can range from three days to two months,[20] so some people may have moved out of the area before developing typhoid and cannot be traced as they either recovered or died without an obituary. Another consideration is that typhoid could be a precipitating factor in someone's death but was not recorded on the death certificate; the *Worthing Gazette* reported that Stanley Elsworth, an 18-year-old apprentice printer from Worthing, died from a lung infection on September 25th at Henfield where he had been sent to recuperate from typhoid[21] – but his death certificate records he died of phthisis (consumption), haemoptysis (spitting up blood) and syncope (fainting).

Mortality Rates by Area and Gender Split:

Table 4 shows that due to its population size, Worthing had the greatest number of typhoid cases and deaths.

	Estimated Population Size	Number of Typhoid Cases	Deaths
Worthing	15270	1261	155
West Worthing	2100	58	14
West Tarring	1070	55	9
Broadwater	787	42	9
Total	**19227**	**1416**	**187**

◀ *Table 4: Number of typhoid cases and deaths by area.*[22]

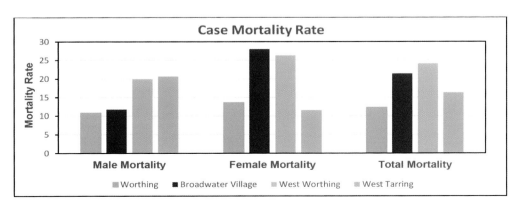

◀ *Fig. 2: Total case mortality by gender for each area, and the total case mortality for all areas – the seven out-of-area deaths not included.*[23]

However, comparing the total typhoid case mortality rate for each area, that is the number of deaths as a proportion of the typhoid cases, shows that Worthing had the lowest mortality rate and West Worthing the highest – see Fig. 2 (final set of columns on the right).

More females than males died in each area, except in West Tarring (Fig. 2). In total, a higher number of females (110) died than males (77). Worthing borough, that is Worthing and West Worthing combined, had an 'excess of females' due to the high number of them employed in lodging houses, private residences and schools.[24] The gender split for the combined population of Worthing borough was 6,874 males to 9,732 females,[25] so it could be argued that this was the reason for more females dying than males. However, when the number of cases in these two areas are split into genders, 9 per 100 males caught typhoid compared to 7 in 100 females;[26] thus fewer females caught typhoid, but with a mortality rate of 14.29 compared to 11.15 for males they were more likely to die.

West Tarring and Broadwater's main areas of employment were fruit growing and agriculture,[27] and they had more even male-to-female population ratios. In the 1891 Census, West Tarring's population was split 544 males to 491 females so this would perhaps account for more males than females dying in West Tarring (Fig. 2). Broadwater had the highest female case mortality rate (Fig. 2), with a population of 483 males compared to 533 females. Of the nine deaths in Broadwater, seven were female of which four were wives; Sarah Butcher, aged 45 years, and Eliza Dorey, aged 29 years, died within a week of each other and were neighbours living at 1 and 3 Bartlett Cottages respectively. Thomson noted that in Broadwater many of the houses were old, and some were badly ventilated and damp with sanitary conditions in 'some respects unsatisfactory'.[28]

Analysis by Age:

Analysing the 194 victims by age shows those in their teens suffered the highest proportion of deaths, with females predominant in this age group. Of note is the high number of 19-year-old females who died, many of them were domestic servants, such as Lilian Allen or Kate Burtenshaw. In an action a newspaper described as criminal recklessness, one female domestic servant died after daring another servant to drink unboiled water with her.[29] In the age group five to ten years, males were affected more, such as Sidney Standing, a general porter's son and Harry Tupper, the son of a chimney sweep. This could be partly due to where they played, the boys at Holy Trinity School were warned 'not to play in the 'sinks' or sewer grates during the drought.'[30] The youngest victim was Winifred Duncan aged four months, and the eldest Helena Bishop, a 76-year-old stonemason's widow. Fig. 3 highlights the fact that the number of deaths sharply decreased from the age of mid-thirty years upwards. These statistics confirm the assertion that it was a 'disease of the young', which was partly due to adults in endemic areas being more resistant to typhoid bacteria than children.[31]

Children under two years are rarely diagnosed with typhoid because symptoms in this age group are 'blurred' and can often be confused with other illnesses.[32] However, in Worthing, four children aged under two years had this recorded as their cause of death. On examination of the child non-typhoid deaths in 1893 from April onwards; 14 children under two years died from diarrhoea and four from gastroenteritis or gastric catarrh, so it is possible that some of these children died from undiagnosed typhoid. Two West Tarring burials were noted as typhoid deaths in the burial register, but the death certificates recorded the cause of death as two months of chronic gastric catarrh in the case of Ernest Laishley, aged five months, and seven days of diarrhoea in the case of Nellie Lindup, aged seven months. There were also indirect deaths caused by typhoid, Elizabeth Gordon, a coachman's wife, caught it while pregnant and died eight days after giving birth to her son Alfred, who due to artificial feeding died two days after she did; while Edward Murrell was out unsupervised watching elephants in a circus procession when he was knocked down by a horse and died of his injuries a few days before his mother Mary died of typhoid.[33]

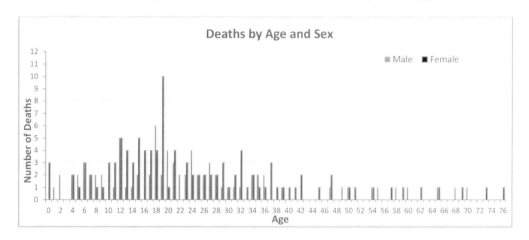

◀ *Fig. 3: Typhoid deaths by age and gender.*

Analysis by occupation and gender:

Analysing the occupations of those who died shows that the men had a wide variety of jobs (Fig. 4). The most affected occupations were labourers and gardeners, reflecting two of the major areas of employment in the town. Most of the gardeners were employed in market gardening as Worthing was the glasshouse capital of Europe, with the first one built from glass used in the 1851 Great Exhibition.[34] Fruits, such as grapes, which were exported to America, vegetables, such as cucumbers, which were purchased by Welsh miners for refreshment down the mines, and flowers, such as chrysanthemums and orchids, were grown.[35] Labourers would either have been market garden labourers or building labourers. Most of these men were breadwinners for their family; Abraham Duffield was a 34-year-old market gardener who died on May 27th leaving six children – one of them three-weeks-old – unprovided for, so a public subscription was started which enabled his wife Eliza to open a small shop.[36]

◀ *Fig. 4: Occupations of those who died – males.*

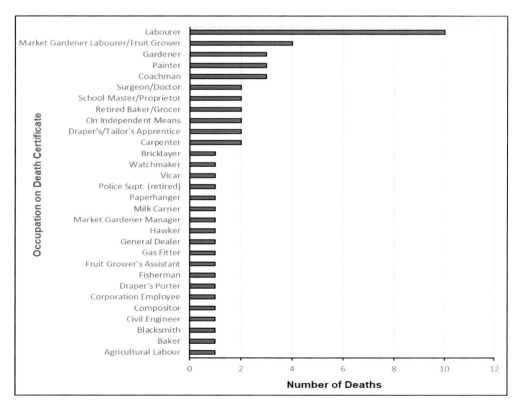

Analysis of female occupations (Fig. 5) shows that many were wives, and a large number were mothers; including Harriet Churcher who died in July, aged 39 years, leaving eight children, two of them under two years of age. Many were employed as domestic servants or housemaids, including Rose Butcher aged 16 years who died in August and Mary Ann Millson, aged 26 years, whose father travelled from Newbury to register her death in July. He was not the only parent who travelled to Worthing to register their child's death – Ellen, Charles Habgood's mother travelled from Upper Norwood as Charles had moved to Worthing to become a draper's apprentice.

Two doctors and two nurses died from typhoid and three schoolteachers died, including Francis Farrant who died in July leaving a pregnant wife.

▶ Fig. 5: Occupations of those who died – females.

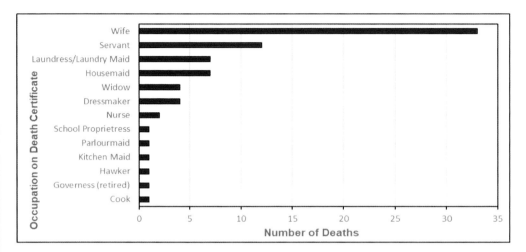

Analysis by Socio-Economic Class:

An analysis of the class occupation of each victim was undertaken using the Social Classification Scheme[37] to ascertain which social-economic class was most affected:

- Class I includes clergy, doctors, engineers, and architects.
- Class II includes retailers, dealers, teachers, agents, and managers.
- Class III includes policemen, bricklayers, painters, and bakers.
- Class IV includes gardeners, servants, brickmakers, and coachmen.
- Class V includes labourers, and hawkers.

If someone was a 'master', then they were an employer and were moved up to Class II, for example, a grocer is allocated to Class III but a grocer master would be in Class II. Occupations were counted only once where there was more than one death in a household; for example, Emily and George Charles, wife and son respectively of Jonathan, a builder's carter; or the Muzzell family, George aged five, and Caroline aged six, children of a brickmaker who died in August followed by their mother Alice in November. The results in Table 5 demonstrate the highest number of victims were in the working classes, particularly amongst the partly skilled working class.

▶ Table 5: Household class occupation.

Class	Number in each	Percentage of deaths
Class I – Professional/Higher Middle Class	9	5.1
Class II – Intermediate/Lower Middle Class	22	12.4
Class III - Skilled Working Class	45	25.4
Class IV – Partly Skilled Working Class	52	29.4
Class V - Unskilled Working Class	49	27.7

Analysis by Areas and Wards:

As Worthing developed, large houses in prime seafront positions were built while a poorer district grew up behind them. The west of the town established large villas while poorer housing was found bordering the railway line.[38] During the course of the epidemic, virtually every street in Worthing had typhoid cases with pockets of infection in the neighbouring parishes, as illustrated by the map below – see Fig. 6.

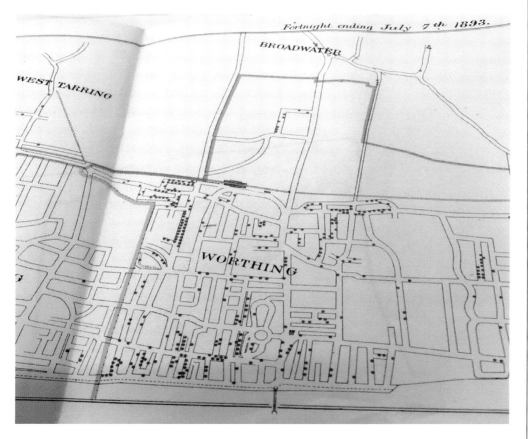

◀ Fig. 6: The spread of typhoid cases at the beginning of July 1893 – out-of-area deaths not included.[39]

Worthing was split into four wards – central, east, north-east and north-west while West Worthing was covered by the west ward. Analysing the addresses of the victims shows central ward had the most typhoid deaths, whereas Broadwater and West Tarring had the lowest (Table 6). However, central ward had nearly three times as many residents as the other wards so when the mortality rate per 1,000 is calculated, the north-west ward had the highest mortality rate of 13.6 followed by the east ward with 10.7. Broadwater village with its nine deaths from such a small population also had a high mortality rate.

Ward	Total Deaths	Estimated Population Size in 1893	Mortality Population Rate Per 1000
Central	57	6280	9.1
East	31	2900	10.7
N-E	25	3000	8.3
N-W	42	3090	13.6
West	14	2100	6.7
Broadwater	9	787	11.4
West Tarring	9	1070	8.4

◀ Table 6: Total deaths, population size, and mortality rate by ward – out of area deaths not included.[40]

An attempt was made to record the rateable value of each victim's house, but the *Worthing Rate Book* for 1893 does not always record house numbers. However,[41] a large enough sample was gained which demonstrates that most of the housing in the north-west and east wards had rateable values under £10.0.0. Central ward had values ranging from £6.0.0. to £84.0.0 which was not only due to its different classes of housing, but because this ward had a lot of hotels and shops; for example, Sarah Fisher, wife of a boot salesman, lived and died at 24, South Street which had a rateable value of £52.0.0 and was a shop, Freeman Hardy & Willis, which they probably lived above. The west ward was a predominantly affluent area and had a low typhoid death rate. Many of those who were wealthy could afford to leave Worthing and did so.[42] Nevertheless, the youngest typhoid victim, Winifred Duncan, aged four months, was the daughter of a man of independent means and lived in this ward in a house called Seaforth with a rateable value of £32.0.0. It is also of note that many of the Heene victims were domestic servants living in rateable houses of £13.0.0. or less.

Fig. 7: On the western side of present-day Clifton Road were some 43 cottages & a Public House, constituting New Town. There were eight deaths attributable to typhoid in this community (WL).

Clusters of Typhoid Deaths:

There were three main clusters of typhoid deaths, all in the poorer areas of town: near the seafront, to the east parallel with the railway line, and to the west of the station (Fig. 8). The latter area had the highest concentration of typhoid deaths with the greatest number of deaths, eight, on Clifton Road which was known as 'New Town' where small, terraced houses had been built in the early nineteenth century to house the 'labouring classes.'[43] The Clifton Road residents were a close-knit community and housed many bricklayers, labourers and gardeners[44] – see Fig. 7.

Parallel roads in this area were also affected badly with seven dying on London Street, six on Howard Street, and six on Orme Road. There was a cluster of deaths near Homefield Park, to the east of the town parallel with the railway line, where eight people died on Newland Road and seven on Station Road – see Table 7.

▶ Table 7: Number of deaths by address and ward.

Address	Number of Deaths	Ward
Clifton Road	8	North-West
London Street	7	North-West
Howard Street	6	North-West
Orme Road	6	North-West
Newland Road	8	North-East
Market Street	7	Central
Chapel Street	5	Central
Station Road	7	East
Ham Arch/Ham Lane	7	East
Park Road	6	East

Figure 8: Ordnance Survey Maps of Worthing & West Worthing 1896 (Godfrey Maps) 64.14 & 64.15. Each spot represents a death, placing on the road not exact due to multiple deaths in some households and unknown position of house numbers.[47]

103

The other cluster of deaths was near the seafront on roads between Paragon Street and the Lifeboat House. During wet weather, the sewers would back up to the bottom of South Street, and during storms would also back up along Montague Street and up branch sewers.[45] Thomson in his report acknowledged that there were clusters of 'spots' and pointed out that these were localities that were the most densely inhabited.[46] Market Street in central ward registered seven deaths including Ann and Annie Lelliott, mother and daughter, at number 15. Ham Arch and Ham Lane suffered seven deaths including four children; nine-month Annie Page, daughter of a fruit-grower labourer, two-year-old Walter Laker, son of a market gardener, and brother and sister, George, aged five years and Caroline, aged six years, as well as their mother Alice Muzzell.

Hospital versus Home Treatment:

At the start of the epidemic, two tents on the lawn in front of the Infirmary were used for cases, but in July when the outbreak escalated, the tents were closed and six temporary fever hospitals in Worthing, one in Broadwater, and two in West Tarring were opened. These gave priority to those aged 10 – 35 years, which confirms the data analysis that the disease was most prevalent in this age group.[48] In total, 485 people were treated in the Infirmary, the tents and the temporary hospitals where 75 people died, compared to 112 people from 931 nursed at home.[49] There was a higher mortality rate amongst those who were admitted to hospital than those who were nursed at home with the total percentage of deaths in hospital 15.5% compared to 12% for those at home. Dr Kelly stated this was not because the hospitals took the worse cases as 'the applications for admission came in too fast for any selection of cases,' but was due to receiving the patients in an exhausted state.[50] He also remarked that the hospitals were overcrowded, but space was less important as the dry weather meant the doors and windows could be left open all day ensuring a good supply of fresh air.[51] A secondary cause of death was often exhaustion and 68 people had this entered on their death certificate; for example, Harriet Page, aged 32 years, died of enteric fever, phthisis and exhaustion in the Iron Chapel (Fig. 9), the temporary hospital in Lyndhurst Road. If people who were sick with typhoid left Worthing they could be prosecuted! Richard Fulden-Taylor was fined 5s. for sending his servant, Eleanor Ade, who was ill with typhoid, to be nursed in Steyning.[52] This did not deter some people. Ellen Broadbridge, servant to a Worthing fishmonger, caught typhoid and returned home to Washington village, seven miles away, in the carrier's cart with her father carrying her the last mile in his arms; sadly she died three weeks later.[53]

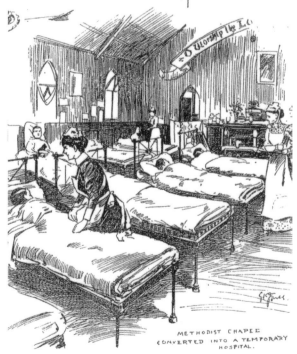

▼ Fig. 9: This artist's impression of life inside the Iron Chapel appeared in the Daily Graphic for August 26th 1893.

METHODIST CHAPEL CONVERTED INTO A TEMPORARY HOSPITAL.

Burial Plots:

Those who died in West Tarring and most of those in West Worthing were buried in their respective parish graveyards. Some victims were buried out-of-the-area, including Alfred Piercy, aged 9 years, whose body was returned to his family and buried in Smethwick Churchyard, Staffordshire[54] and Sarah Ellis, aged 59 years, a school proprietor who was buried in Norwood Cemetery.[55] However, most victims were buried in Broadwater and Worthing Cemetery where there were three categories of interment (Fig. 10). The cheapest was Section A (10s.6d.), which was also where people were buried at the expense of the Poor Law Union, Section B (15s.), or the most expensive Section C (£1.1.0.).[56] Headstones were an extra expense, but there is no record of these, and many stones are illegible or have disappeared. Analysing the burial plot of each victim according to the ward they lived in shows the east ward appears to be the poorest area with only two people buried in the 'B'

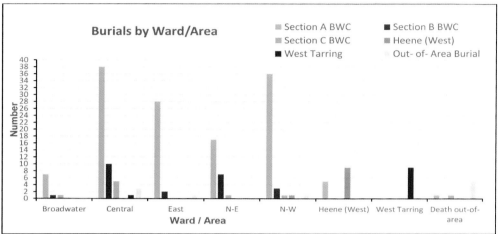

◀Fig. 10: Burial plots via ward, village or out-of-area split into Broadwater and Worthing Cemetery (BWC) sections, and Heene, West Tarring and out-of-area burial grounds.

Section: Caroline Burrell, aged 21 years, a laundrymaid, and Henry Alabaster, aged 65 years, a retired master baker. Central ward by comparison has the most people buried in both 'B' and 'C' sections, including William Rich, aged 47 years, a paper hanger. This reflects its population size and mix of housing. West Worthing (Heene) consisted of better housing and was for the most part a prosperous area, however, five victims from this area were not buried in Heene burial ground but were interred in Broadwater and Worthing Cemetery in the cheapest plots; they were three domestic servants and a brother and sister; Harry Beach, aged 17 years, a milk carrier and his sister Kate, aged 9 years. A total of 132 people were interred in the cheapest plots, with most victims buried in Section A7 (99), reinforcing the data analysis that most victims were from the lower classes. Nevertheless, the purchase of some higher priced plots, 23 in 'B' and nine in 'C' demonstrates that not all the victims were from the lower classes. In total, 164 victims were buried in Broadwater and Worthing Cemetery. A gravedigger[57] at the time recollected how they were often digging graves from 4am to 8pm which gave rise to a popular rumour, which even reached New Zealand, that the dead were being buried at night to cover up the true scale of the epidemic.[58]

Conclusion:

The known number of victims of the Worthing typhoid epidemic is 194, but the total might be higher due to the unknown number of out-of-area deaths. There may have been undiagnosed cases and deaths in young children, and the epidemic was also responsible for several indirect deaths. The typhoid epidemic particularly affected the young, especially in the age groups five to 25 years. With over 1,400 typhoid cases, most streets in Worthing were affected, with concentrations of typhoid deaths, particularly in the Clifton Road area which housed many labourers and gardeners in terraced housing. Some families lost multiple family members; husbands lost wives and vice versa, children lost one or both parents, and children died, in some cases, parents lost more than one child. The data analysis has shown that the *Pall Mall Gazette* was correct when it stated that the highest proportion of deaths was in the lower classes. The poor could not afford to leave Worthing while the wealthy could and did escape from the town. Alice Humphrey's stonemason father carved on her gravestone that 'fierce diseases wait around to hurry mortals' home', but nowadays early treatment with antibiotics usually allows the disease to be quickly beaten. Identifying the victims has enabled data analysis to be performed on their statistics which gives a better understanding of the typhoid epidemic and most importantly the people themselves.

1 'Typhoid Fever at Worthing', London Evening Standard, July 24th 1893, p.3

2 'Fever-Stricken Worthing', Pall Mall Gazette, July 24th 1893, p.7

3 Thomson, T, Report to the Local Government Board on an Epidemic of Enteric Fever in the Borough of Worthing and in the Villages of Broadwater and West Tarring (London, 1894), p.2. Thomson commissioned a census mid-1893.

4 Friends of Broadwater and Worthing Cemetery, The Spanish Flu Epidemic (2015), p.5

5 University of Portsmouth, Worthing MB through time | Population Statistics | Total Population, A Vision of Britain through Time (2009–2017) www.visionofbritain.org.uk/unit/10023830/cube/TOT_POP [accessed June 12th 2021]

6 Hare, C, Worthing - a History, Riot and Respectability in a Seaside Town (Chichester, 2008) pp.107–108

7 Fifty-ninth Annual report of the registrar-general 1896 (BPP,1897), p.ciii

8 Burial Registers for Broadwater & Worthing Cemetery, St Mary's Broadwater, Heene Cemetery, and St Andrew's West Tarring, West Sussex Register Office. Christ Chuch figures compiled using Bishops' Transcripts, Monumental Inscriptions and a Parish Clerk's Record Book, West Sussex Register Office.

9 Kelly, C, Annual Report of the Condition of the Combined Sanitary District of West Sussex 1893 (Worthing, 1893) p.124

10 Kelly, C, Report on the Epidemic of Enteric Fever in 1893, p.9. T. Thomson, Report to the Local Government Board on an Epidemic of Enteric Fever, p.2 records 1411 but does not include the five cases reported in December.

11 Kelly, C, Report on the Epidemic of Enteric Fever in 1893, p.11

12 Thomson, T, Report to the Local Government Board on an Epidemic of Enteric Fever, p.4

13 Thomson, T, Report to the Local Government Board on an Epidemic of Enteric Fever, p.2 and C. Kelly, Report on the Epidemic of Enteric Fever in 1893, p.11

14 Porta, M & Last, J, 'Typhoid (enteric fever)', A Dictionary of Public Health (2 ed.) (Oxford, 2018)

15 Barnett, R, 'Typhoid Fever', The Lancet, 388 (2016), p.2467

16 LeBaron, C & Taylor, D, 'Typhoid Fever', in Kiple, K (ed.), The Cambridge World History of Human Disease, (Cambridge, 1993) pp. 1071–1077

17 Kelly,C. Report on the Epidemic of Enteric Fever in 1893, p.11

18 LeBaron, C. & D. Taylor, 'Typhoid Fever', in K. Kiple (ed.), p.1073

19 Kelly,C. Annual Report of the Condition of the Combined Sanitary District of West Sussex 1893 (Worthing, 1893) p.122

20 World Health Organisation, Typhoid Fever, 2022, www.emro.who.int/health-topics/typhoid-fever/introduction.html [accessed December 27th 2022].

21 'Funeral of Mr S.J.Elsworth', Worthing Gazette, October 4th 1893, p.5]

22 Kelly, C, 1893 Sanitary District Report p.136 for Ward figures, Thomson, T, Enteric Fever Report for Broadwater and West Tarring estimated population p.2. Case figures from Table 1, death figures from Typhoid Research Project

23 Kelly, C, Report on the Epidemic of Enteric Fever in 1893, p.11

24 Kelly, C, Annual Report of the Condition of the Combined Sanitary District of West Sussex 1893 (Worthing, 1893) p.122

25 Kelly, C, Report on the Epidemic of Enteric Fever in 1893, p.11. Kelly has used 1891 Census figures.

26 Ibid

27 Thomson, T, Report to the Local Government Board on an Epidemic of Enteric Fever, p.3

28 Ibid, p.8

29 Christian Herald, September 7th 1893, Worthing Reference Library Bound Collection of Newspaper Cuttings, shelf mark 614.49

30 Headteacher: Logbook, 'Holy Trinity Church of England School' (1891–1912), July 6th 1893, West Sussex Record Office, E\218N\12

31 LeBaron, C & Taylor, D, 'Typhoid Fever', in K. Kiple (ed.), p.1072

32 Ibid, p.1073

33 'Going out to see the Circus', Worthing Gazette, August 2nd 1893, p.8

34 Baggs, A P, Currie, C R J, Elrington, C R, Keeling, S M, and Rowland, A M, 'Worthing Economic history', in A History of the County of Sussex: Volume 6 Part 1, Bramber Rape (Southern Part), ed. Hudson, T P (London, 1980), pp. 109-114. British History Online www.british-history.ac.uk/vch/sussex/vol6/pt1/pp109-114 [accessed 13 June 2021] pp.109-114

35 Linfield, A G junior, 'The Worthing and District Glasshouse Industry', in Migeod, F (ed.), Worthing A Survey of Times Past and Present (Worthing, 1938) p.137–138

36 Woolgar, M, 'Afflicted Worthing: Some Victims of the Epidemic', Journal of the West Sussex Archives Society, 79 (2011) p.15

37 Appendix 1: 'The Social Classification Scheme', link.springer.com/content/pdf/bbm:978-0-230-37321-1/1.pdf [accessed 13 June 2021].

38 Brookfield, H, 'Worthing: A Study of a Modern Coastal Town', The Town Planning Review, 23 (1952) pp.150–153

39 Thomson, T, Report to the Local Government Board on an Epidemic of Enteric Fever, p.67

40 See Endnote 21

41 Worthing Rate Book 1893, West Sussex Record Office, BO/WO/35/4/5

42 Sussex Daily News, August 10th 1893, Worthing Reference Library Bound Collection of Newspaper Cuttings, shelf mark 614.49

43 Hare, C, Worthing - a History, Riot and Respectability in a Seaside Town, (Chichester, 2008) p.33

44 Census 1891, Worthing, RG12/837

45 Thomson, T, Report to the Local Government Board on an Epidemic of Enteric Fever, p.9

46 Ibid p.7

47 Emily Sanders, aged 21 years, domestic servant not included as home address unknown. Some addresses in West Tarring, Broadwater, and Heene not included due to the scope of the map or due to unknown addresses, for example, James Cottages, Heene is an unknown location.

48 Kelly, C, Report on the Epidemic of Enteric Fever in 1893, p.49

49 Ibid, pp.51–52

50 Ibid, p.51

51 Ibid, p.49

52 'Prosecution at Steyning', West Sussex County Times, September 2nd 1893, p.7

53 Lidbetter, L 'Personal Recollection Letter,' (1977), West Sussex Record Office, MP1390

54 Smethwick Old Church, Staffordshire Monumental Inscriptions

55 Woolgar, M, 'Afflicted Worthing Research

56 Long's Worthing Directory (Worthing, 1892), p.41

57 Worthing Herald November 20th 1953 identifies him as Frank Horner

58 'Typhoid Fever', Lyttelton Times, Christchurch, July 25th 1893, p.5. '80 deaths from typhoid fever..... The victims are buried at night, and all excursion trains to the town are stopped.'

Chapter 8
Snippets

Gathered by Mary Mckeown

In August 1893, a well-known character called Martin Pennifold, was charged with being a lunatic wandering at large in Lancing. He had been to see the mayor of Worthing about a remedy he had for the fever, and it was his duty as a philanthropist and a Christian not to keep the recipe to himself. He asked the magistrate to make a note of it, which he did. It was 3oz of cream of tartar, 12 grains of turkey rhubarb and 1 pint and a quarter of pure cold water. He then went on to describe how to make his beverage.

After his conduct report was read out it was ordered that he be taken to Haywards Heath Asylum.[1]

****

The Heene Day School Log records:

'**May 19th** – 29 children absent due to sickness... three cases of typhoid fever reported.

August 15th – notices were sent to parents on Monday to ascertain the cause of absence:

22 cases of typhoid fever reported, several sick, and a great many absent through fear.'[2]

****

Mr Lorenzo Ferrari, opened a free soup kitchen in the old drill hall in Bath Place, for the people of the town during the epidemic. Mr. Ferrari was the proprietor of the Imperial Restaurant, in South Street, which later became The Ship.[3]

****

Mr Henry Joseph Phillips of 42, Clifton Rd died in 1952 at the age of 84. One of his most vivid memories was when he distributed drinking water during the epidemic using horse drawn vehicles.[4]

****

Mr Frank Horner of 32 Marlowe Road recalled in 1950 when he started as a gravedigger in 1890 at Broadwater Cemetery. 'We had our worst time during the typhoid epidemic from May to September 1893. Sometimes we began our task at 4 o'clock in the morning and finished at eight at night.'[5]

****

On October 25th 1894, Mr Edward Harrison was made the first Freeman of the Borough. This honour was in recognition of his services to the town during the epidemic. When the search for a new water supply to the town was desperately needed, Mr. Harrison believed that there was a sufficient supply of water under his land at Lyons Farm to supply the town, and he placed it freely at the Corporation's disposal. This undoubtedly saved many lives.[6]

****

Mr F D Butler of Ferring, recalled how during the epidemic he was a boarder at Grafton House School. 'When the typhoid came the school was closed and was transferred to Bexhill–on-Sea.'[7]

****

'TYPHOID IN BUTTER

Nurses would do well to remember the fact which has just been made public, that an epidemic of typhoid fever has been traced to the use of butter made from milk from an infected farm. It has been well known, of course, for years, that milk was a common carrier of the disease, so that there is nothing astonishing in the new discovery. But it emphasizes the necessity for caution and investigation in the event of an outbreak of the fever without any very evident cause. In this connection also it is well to remember that ice, even when to all appearance pure, has been found to contain germs capable of developing disease, and should, therefore, not be allowed to come in contact with food or drink. Probably, in many cases, illness, which has been attributed to taking iced drinks, was, in fact, due to the presence of disease germs, and not, as has often thought, to the cold.'[8]

****

On August 17th 1893 Kate Dunn died. Her schoolmistress recorded in the school log book, 'Kate Dunn, who has been ill only a week died this afternoon. She was a quiet and intelligent child and one of the brightest of her class.' Later, on 19th September another school entry reveals that Kate's sister Amelia had 'failed with fever'. Amelia was much luckier than her younger sister and survived the fever.[9]

****

'Three Promotions to Glory from Worthing. During the last three weeks the Angel of Death has been busy at Worthing. Amongst the victims he has claimed are three who were soldiers of The Salvation Army. Their names are as follows, Sister Lottie Graham, Sergt-Major W. Stace and Brother Ernest Braby.'[10]

****

Miss Valetta Shout recalled how as a young nurse she volunteered throughout the epidemic at the Parish Room, Broadwater. Here, the patients were nursed on the floor until beds could be procured. The work was strenuous, all the patient's milk had to be boiled and beef tea made at the Cricketers Inn had to be fetched from there. The nurses were housed in East Worthing and driven back and forth to the temporary hospital in a little pony carriage.[11]

****

'The Nurses employed at the Travellers Rest temporary hospital desire to express their best thanks to all the kind friends who have given them drives, free passes to the Pier, gifts of fruit and flowers, and who have entertained them at their houses during their sojourn in Worthing.'[12]

'Mr J West, Heene House, West Worthing. BEGS TO GIVE NOTICE, That owing to the continuance of typhoid fever in Worthing. He has TEMPORARILY REMOVED his pupils to FOREST HOUSE, LANCING, SUSSEX.'[13]

****

'The following is a copy of the testimonial, which will be given to each of the nurses...

Worthing District Nursing Association, Special Branch;

The Committee of the Special Branch of the Worthing District Nursing Association, and Medical Practitioners whose cases she has had charge of during the Epidemic of Typhoid Fever, wish to express their very high opinion of the services of Nurse _____, she has been kind and attentive to the large number of patients under her care, thoroughly conscientious and painstaking in the discharge of her very arduous duties, and has proved herself in every way a reliable and efficient Nurse – Worthing, October 21st 1893.'[14]

****

'GRATITUDE

To the Editor of the Gazette:

Dear Sir, I shall be glad if you will allow me to state in your paper how grateful I am to all who have shown so much kindness to my husband during his long and serious illness from typhoid. He received the best attention from the Doctors, Matron and Nurses at the Richmond House Hospital, and has now been enabled to go to the Convalescent Home in York Terrace; and I feel that I cannot sufficiently express my thanks to all who have ministered to him and assisted in his recovery.

I am, Sir,

Yours very truly,

Lizzie Brown

4, Elliott's Cottages,

North Street

September 19th, 1893.

The father and mother of the patient, Thomas and Hannah Brown, writing from the same address, also wish to express through our columns their gratitude to all concerned.'[15]

****

'**12th May 1893** - Lily Bridger and Annie Dale sick with typhoid fever.

19th May 1893 - Maggie Bridger and Agnes Winfield are fresh cases of typhoid fever.

2nd June 1893 - Lily Osborne- pupil teacher ill with typhoid fever, but a mild case.

6th October 1893 - Florrie Deadman failed with fever.

24th November 1893 - Ruth Warren died on 21st of typhoid fever. The girls brought flowers and money for a wreath at their own request.'[16]

****

Mr James Town offered the use of a brake twice, so that the nurses 'may be taken out for an airing'.[17]

****

In September 1893, a notice was now being exhibited daily at the foot of the Town Hall steps. It gave the number of fresh cases officially notified in the previous 24 hours.[18]

IMPORTANT !

All Drinking Water **MUST** still be BOILED.

Water supplied to the Tanks is NOT intended to be used for Horses and Cattle, but for Drinking and Cooking purposes only.

CHARLES C. COOK,
Chairman Sanitary Committee.

August 24th, 1893. [19]

****

'UNSPARING GENEROSITY

To The Editor of the Worthing Intelligencer:

Dear Sir, Will you allow me through your paper to thank the Committee of the Sick Poor Fund for their gift to me, for expenses incurred through the death of my wife at West Worthing, from the fever – which she caught at one of the Convalescent Homes to which she went daily to attend to domestic duties. I know that the Committee now intend paying arrears of rent and rent in advance to the amount of several pounds to those applying, although there has been no case of fever in some of their houses. I think this is a marked contrast to their sparing generosity in awarding only £1 10s. in my own case; for – as a journeyman baker on about £1 a week – with funeral and extra expenses for a woman to attend the children, this did not go far.

Surely those suffering directly from the fever should have the first and strongest claim on the Fund?

E. J. COMPTON'

After the death of his wife Mary, Mr. Compton also suffered the loss of his 15-month-old daughter, Frances, on December 5th 1893. Frances' death was recorded as being from Dentition Diarrhoea.[20]

****

'BREAD AND PURE WATER

To the Editor of the Worthing Intelligencer:

DEAR SIR, A report is current that I manufacture my bread from the Worthing water. I beg to contradict that statement most emphatically, as the water I use is from the same well that has been in use now 30 years, and where the well water is drank we have not a single case of typhoid in the whole village – A sufficient proof of its purity.

I remain,

Your obedient servant,

J B KNOWLES.

South House, Broadwater.'[21]

****

'ILLNESS OF THE VICAR OF WEST TARRING

We deeply regret to hear that the Rector of West Tarring is laid aside with illness, contracted during his devoted administration to his people in the present epidemic.'[22]

****

EXTRACTS FROM CHRIST CHURCH SCHOOL LOG BOOK

'**8th May 1893** – Edith Pellett is taken with typhoid fever and will not be at school for some weeks.

29th May 1893 – Rose May very ill with typhoid fever, will be absent some weeks to come, she has been frequently absent through ill health.

10th June or July 1893 – Attendance smaller today, John Street and Frank Hobbs have typhoid fever.

14th August 1893 – School reopened this morning with very small attendances owing to typhoid fever, which is raging fearfully throughout the town.

21st August 1893 – Edith Brazier has leave of absence, as her sister is to be buried today.

4th September 1893 – Freddy Bennett and Lizzie Wingfield returned today having been absent since before the holidays.

18th September 1893 – John Street who has been dangerously ill with typhoid has gone away for a few weeks.

20th September 1893 – Edith Deadman failed with typhoid this week and Louisa Hunt is also laid up.

27th September 1893 – Albert Massey has failed today with typhoid, he has been attending regularly lately and hoped to pass on with other boys to the boys school.

2nd October 1893 – Annie Edwards is gone away for a month to stay with her grandmother in Devonshire.

20th October 1893 – Daisy and Violet Frances and Willie Percy have left school as their parents have gone from the town.

November 1893 – The Paceys and Keileys are removing to another part of the town, therefore will attend the schools nearer their homes.

19th February 1894 – Willie Luff and Louisa Hunt have left school, their parents having left the town.'[23]

****

The patients who were nursed at the Richmond House Hospital during the epidemic were invited to spend a social evening on January 9th 1894. Tea, music and recitations were all included free of charge.[24]

****

In 1952, Mr George Town recalled:

'The place was deserted. You could have fired a shot down the front without hitting anyone.' He added that 'the disease was so widespread that some of his horses got it and had to be given whisky and new laid eggs to keep them alive.'[25]

****

'A FURTHER APPEAL TO THE HASTINGS PEOPLE

The Rector of St Leonards-on-Sea, after returning home from helping his son at Christ Church last Sunday week, wrote the following letter to the Hasting papers:

THE DISTRESS AT WORTHING.

To the Editor of the Observer.

Sir, I have just returned from Worthing, where I was officiating Sunday last, and after what I saw and heard there, I wish to add my testimony as to the dire distress which has overtaken this sister watering place on our own Sussex coast. The place seems literally deserted. All along the Front the white bills in the windows tell of vacant "apartments" belonging to those who are still trying to make a living in this way, and sadder still "to be let or sold," telling of those who have struggled and failed. Hundreds of lodging house keepers are reduced to the greatest straits. Hundreds of young men and women have been turned out of their employment in shops, and hundreds of residents have left the place. I heard for instance of seven boarding schools attending one church, three another, and there are several more, which have been removed to other towns (one at least to St. Leonards). This of course, greatly affects the artizan (sic) and poor classes. So that at the very time when the epidemic has cut down the bread winners, or deprived them of work, there are scarcely any of the upper class to help them in their need. Assistance, then, must come from outsiders, and I trust that Hastings and St. Leonards will not be behind Brighton, Eastbourne, etc., in liberally rendering this assistance.

All contributions should be sent to our esteemed Mayor, Dr Croucher. They will then be forwarded to the Mayor of Worthing, and properly administered to carefully investigated cases which have been recommended by the clergy and ministers of the town.

Yours truly,

J Awdry Jamieson.

The Rectory, St. Leonards-on-Sea'[26]

****

Henry Silvester, a retired superintendent in the West Sussex Constabulary, died in the early morning of Saturday 19th August 1893 and was buried the same day.[27]

****

TOWER BREWERY,
WORTHING.

IMPORTANT NOTICE.

OWING to the supposed cause of the present unfortunate epidemic in our midst, I feel it is desirable, for the satisfaction of my customers, that I should assure them it is absolutely impossible to brew either ALE OR STOUT unless the WATER USED BOILS FURIOUSLY FOR SEVERAL HOURS.

As Tea and Coffee (made with water which has just reached the boiling point) are consumed daily, and with impunity, the fact that all water used in the production of ALE AND STOUT is of necessity boiled for so great a length of time, must satisfy everyone that such liquors are produced under perfectly satisfactory conditions.

H. CHAPMAN.

Copy of Letter received from Dr. GOSTLING.—

21st July, 1893.

DEAR SIR,

You ask me if the boiling which takes place in the process of brewing (and which I understand to be from two to three hours) is sufficient to destroy any germs which may be in the water?

I can say, without hesitation, that it certainly is.

I am, yours faithfully,

W. AYTON GOSTLING, M.D.

Barningham, West Worthing.

[28]

****

'SEA TRIP IN AID OF WORTHING

The steamer Princess May will make a special afternoon trip from the West Pier, Brighton, into the Channel to view the shipping tomorrow, the proceeds to be given to the Worthing Relief Fund. The start will be made at 2.45, the steamer returning about six o'clock. These Channel trips are among the most interesting of the Princess May's many journeys.'[29]

'LIBELLOUS STATEMENTS.

Dear Sir, - Will you kindly permit me, through the medium of your paper, to refute a statement that has been circulated to the effect that I have been a recipient of the Mayor's Sick Poor Fund.

I have been a great sufferer from the unfortunate epidemic but I would never accept assistance from a Fund raised, as I believe, for the relief of those in actual distress.

Unfortunately I have not been able to discover the author of the malicious rumour or I should have taken other steps to free myself from the odium thus sought to be cast on me.

I am, dear Sir,

Yours faithfully,

J B WHITINGTON.

Montague Street,

December 7th 1893'[30]

****

'... As a matter of course the tone of Mr. Woodruff's speech about the distress of Worthing was sympathetic and kindly. Having recalled the chief features of the calamity, he mentioned a case that had come within his own experience in which a promising young man in the Indian Civil Service went down to Worthing whilst on leave of absence, took the fever, was removed to a London Hospital and died within a few days. No doubt, he added, there were many cases of that kind which had not been reported...'[31]

****

'A PUBLIC DANGER

...Under these circumstances we desire to point out the serious peril involved in the visits of large numbers of persons, not only from Brighton but from London, and elsewhere by rail to the fever swept town. Many of these are children, and are taken to the town in a very reprehensible defiance of the peril they run. The Worthing town authorities appear disposed to remain silent on the subject, it therefore, becomes the duty of the Press to warn the general public of the danger existing there...'[32]

****

'TORCHLIGHT PROCESSION AT POLEGATE

The members of the Polegate Bonfire Society have decided to have a torchlight procession on Wednesday night. Collecting boxes will be carried, and the whole of the proceeds will be handed over to the Mayor of Worthing's Relief Fund. Members of the Cricket Club and Slate Club will take part in the procession.'[33]

****

'... The Corporation is now thoroughly alive to the danger, but have been very incautious in the past. An outbreak of diphtheria in a ladies school, which took place previously to the outbreak of typhoid, had been kept quiet... There are many cases of school children who have been attacked after drinking unfiltered water from a public fountain. ... The Town Clerk of Worthing informs us that the statement that the victims of the typhoid epidemic have been buried at midnight is untrue. He declares six o'clock in the evening to be the latest hour at which a funeral has taken place.'[34]

****

'FOOTBALL

Like everything else in Worthing, the cricket season has suffered from the terrible scourge of the town, for, many teams absolutely refusing to come to the place even for an afternoon, quite half the matches arranged by the Clubs have fallen through. Now the fever is abating and confidence is being restored, footballers are hoping for a renewal of the interest that was last year evinced in Worthing's contests. On Saturday a scratch match heralded the advent of the winter game... It is too early as yet, however, to form any estimate of the abilities of the men – football itself seems out of place so near such a summer as we have had.'[35]

****

'THE WORTHING EPIDEMIC

... So widespread is the area of the epidemic that there is hardly a street in Worthing in which cases are not to be found. In most of the few tenement houses the outbreak has visited every apartment. It has been found impossible to find hospital accommodation for a large proportion of the sufferers, who were, therefore, treated at their own homes. There is no truth whatever in the statement made that infected houses and localities are indicated by the hoisting of the black flag. The blinds of the houses are simply drawn down and the knockers on the doors wrapped in soft material to deaden the sound.'[36]

****

'A VISIT TO WORTHING by Rev W E Sellers

I have just been to Worthing for the Sunday School Anniversary, and perhaps some tidings of that fever stricken town may be interesting to the readers of the Methodist Recorder... Iron tanks with the inscription "Drinking Water," which are filled by water carts every day, are at every corner. Sallow–faced, short–haired convalescents abound in the streets and on the sea front. There is only one topic of conversation. Everyone has much to tell you about the experiences of the past. Into most homes sickness has entered...

Our own Church has suffered seriously. In our Sunday School over sixty children out of a total of about a hundred and fifty have been attacked, and of these six have died.

On Sunday last many of the school children were arranged on the platform around me, and it was pathetic to see the little yellow faces and the closely cropped hair. ...'[37]

****

'A VICTIM OF THE EPIDEMIC:

A lovely maiden, who had not yet seen
Her nineteenth summer all its glory shed,
To the fever – stricken city, with no dread
Of ill, came, full of life and joy, from green
Fields and fresh breezy hills, to where between
Down and broad sea pure health its bright home made.
But on the town a sudden sickness preyed;
Death spread its paw where festive joy had been:-
All were not struck down. There her sister dwelt –
By an elder sister's side the sweet girl felt
Secure from danger – But, one sultry day,
They shared some treacherous beverage – Soon the pest
On the younger sister did its fierce claws lay –
And – while we grieve – she soars among the blest.   C.W.'[38]

---

1 Extracted from Sussex Daily News, August 17th 1893, WOR 614.49 Typhoid Cuttings Book
2 A Brief Story of Heene, compiled by Muriel G Huxley-Williams, August 1973
3 Extracted from Worthing Herald, August 31st 1951
4 Extracted from Worthing Herald, November 7th 1952
5 Extracted from Worthing Herald, December 29th 1950
6 Extracted from Worthing Gazette, June 9th 1926
7 Extracted from Worthing Herald, December 17th 1948

8 *Nursing Record & Hospital World, October 14th 1893*
9 *Christ Church School log book, WSRO E218F/12/1, E218F/12/3, Ancestry*
10 *The War Cry, August 26th 1893, WOR 614.49*
11 *Extracted from Worthing Gazette, June 17th 1931*
12 *Worthing Intelligencer, September 23rd 1893*
13 *Morning Post, September 2nd 1893*
14 *Worthing Intelligencer, October 21st 1893*
15 *Worthing Gazette, September 20th 1893*
16 *Christ Church School log book, WSRO E218F/12/3*
17 *Extracted Worthing Intelligencer July 22nd 1893*
18 *Extracted from Worthing Gazette, September 13th 1893*
19 *West Sussex Past Pictures, POS/WSL/POS000011*
20 *Worthing Intelligencer, October 7th 1893, Death Certificate*
21 *Worthing Intelligencer, July 22nd 1893*
22 *Worthing Intelligencer, September 9th 1893*
23 *Christ Church School log book, WRSO E218F/12/1*
24 *Extracted from Worthing Gazette, January 3rd 1894*
25 *Worthing Herald August 22nd 1952*
26 *Worthing Gazette, October 4th 1893*
27 *Worthing Gazette, August 23rd 1893, Death Certificate, BWC Burial Records*
28 *Typhoid Cuttings Folder, Worthing Library*
29 *Sussex Daily News, September 4th 1893, WOR 614.49*
30 *Worthing Intelligencer, December 9th 1893*
31 *Brighton Guardian and Hove Recorder, August 30th 1893*
32 *Brighton Guardian and Hove Recorder, July 19th 1893*
33 *Sussex Daily News, September 4th 1893, WOR 614.49*
34 *Sun, July 22nd 1893, WOR 614.49*
35 *Sussex Daily News, September 11th 1893, WOR 614.49*
36 *Morning Leader, July 24th 1893, WOR 614.49*
37 *Methodist Recorder, November 16th 1893, WOR 614.49*
38 *Worthing Intelligencer, August 19th 1893*

THE WATER CHASE

(Published in *The Worthing Intelligencer* on 22nd July 1893)

Some Aldermen and Councillors
Who deemed themselves o'erwise
Set out one afternoon
To find a water prize.

Some carried their umbrellas,
And one a magic wand;
No springs they found to cheer them –
Only a dirty pond.

The country round they scoured in vain,
They walked the hills about,
Through drizzling mist and showers
Still they wandered in and out.

But one cried "Halt! I'm sure I felt
Water in my shoe.
Let's dig a little hole, and see
What Councillors can do!"

"This soil is surely chalky!
Should below this be a well?
I thought that you were clever men.
Can't any of you tell?"

He took a spade, dug down a foot –
The others they dug too –
Twas an enterprising puddle
That had filtered through his shoe.
He raised the rod aloft, and cried,

"O let us stop and think;
Tis – water, water everywhere,
But none that's fit to drink?"

They shrugged their shoulders, shook their heads,
And rattled all their brains,
And tried to talk of strata,
And of lands that have no drains.

No scientist had gone with them,
Their hearts were very sore;
So they gathered up their waterproofs
And trotted home once more.

Oh, pardon, if on minds like these
We have to cast a slur,
And expect some wiser doings
Some lucky day next year.

Now let us learn a moral
From these estimable folk.
We are not all geologists –
Drinking sewage is no joke.

And if our Town's unhealthy,
If we grumble loud and long –
And we have to pay the piper
For the burden of our song –
Let's seek some wiser heads than these
To rectify the wrong.

ANONYMOUS

Chapter 9

Postscript

By Colin Reid

How can we make sense of what happened in Worthing back in 1893, what lessons were learned at the time and are there any parallels with our recent/current experience with the coronavirus pandemic?

As a result of the work of the Typhoid Research Project, we now know the names of 194 people whose demise – as recorded on their death certificates – was attributed to infection with *Salmonella* Typhi during the period from April to December 1893. All four of us suspect the death toll was higher. For example, we know that Stanley Elsworth had travelled from Worthing to Henfield to recuperate from 'an attack of typhoid' and yet there was no mention of that infection on his death certificate;[1] the *Brighton Guardian and Hove Recorder* speaks about 'a promising young man in the Indian Civil Service (who) went down to Worthing whilst he was on leave of absence, took the fever, was removed to a London Hospital, and died within a few days' [his identity is unknown] and that report goes on to say 'no doubt, there were many cases of that kind which had not been reported.'[2] In Worthing itself, Caroline Nelson considers possible under-reporting for infants under two years of age: death was attributed to 'diarrhoea', or two examples in West Tarring where the family and vicar clearly considered typhoid was a factor,[A] or two deaths (Alfred Gordon and Edward Murrell) that may not have occurred but for the presence of typhoid in the town. In chapter 7, Caroline Nelson may well have (but not certainly) discovered the identity of victim 195 in Caroline Annie Vaughan who died of typhoid in Washington aged 19 years and had been a servant in Worthing in 1891. The search goes on!... In his report, Dr Kelly says he received 1,416 notifications of typhoid infection for Worthing, West Worthing, West Tarring and Broadwater between April and December 1893 but was he privy to all of the seven victims who died 'out of area'? For example, it is inconceivable that the

---

[A] *In the West Tarring burial register it was recorded that typhoid was the cause of death for Ernest Laishley and Nellie Lindup, but that was not borne out by their death certificates.*

parents of 15-year-old Gordon Chaplin would have returned him to his school in Cranleigh if they or Dr Kelly were aware of his infection.

Anyone reading this book near the time of its publication must make comparisons with the nation's experience of Covid-19. While Baroness Hallett, chairing the UK Covid-19 Inquiry has been given no deadline for reporting her findings, Drs Kelly and Thomson published their comprehensive reports within seven months of the Worthing typhoid epidemic ending. How can the reader not think of the conduct of such luminaries as Johnson, Cummings, Hancock and others during the Covid crisis, when they read Chris Hare's account of 'the Forty Thieves' during and after the typhoid epidemic; or consider the temerity of Councillor Captain Fraser joining with Fereday in criticising the work of the 'Mayor's Relief Fund' committee when he attended less than 10% of their meetings because he deemed it safer to live in Brighton while the epidemic raged?

The typhoid epidemic had a profound impact on everyday life in Worthing. Once it became clear it wasn't short-lived and was overwhelming normal support systems, relief funds were established to aid the sick poor, labourers, lodging house keepers, small traders, fly proprietors, bath-chairmen, boatmen and many others. The Grafton Road soup kitchen went into overdrive with other such establishments opened. Many of the sick were nursed at home supported by district nurses and a network of temporary hospitals and convalescent homes were opened. These provisions – managed by local bodies – appear to have been able to respond in a flexible and timely manner; and compare favourably with the Government's response to Covid-19 both financially and in the establishment of 'Nightingale Hospitals' and 'eat out to help out'.

Back in 1893, there was no television, radio or social media for the authorities to contend with, but local and national newspapers including residents' letters and local agitators such as Rev Joseph Lancaster (cf Marcus Rashford) provided robust comments on delivery. The conduct of Boris Johnson during the Covid crisis contributed to his downfall as prime minister and, in a similar way, those whose behaviour was exemplary in Worthing in 1893 – such as the Linfields – found favour electorally.

It is humbling to read of nurses volunteering to come to Worthing to support victims of typhoid, just as it was humbling to hear of care staff, in 2020/21, moving into homes for the elderly to provide safe care for residents or of nurses and other health staff continuing to care for patients without adequate 'Personal Protective Equipment (PPE)'. In both instances, those on the front-line were putting their own lives at risk and, indeed, some paid with their lives.

While the headline figure of 194 deaths from typhoid in Worthing in just nine months ensures this epidemic remained a talking point for all those who lived through it, the impact went far beyond that. As Chris Hare commented, some who survived were very ill for weeks and months after being infected. In 1950, for example, Lionel J Redgrave Cripps recalled: 'When a small boy, I well remember the disastrous epidemic of typhoid fever in Worthing…(which) claimed me as one of its victims – I was most critically ill for several months. (I) recovered although given up by three doctors.'[3] His education and that of so many others was disrupted as the school log books testify and, in the private sector, as reported in *Steyne School Autumn Magazine* for 1925: '(Steyne School) was, we believe, the only private school that remained open during the whole of the period. For a long time, Worthing was under a cloud, and passed through some difficult years before regaining her former prosperity.'[4] Everyday leisure pursuits and sports were curtailed – not least because of the reluctance of competitors and spectators to visit the town. So, talking about his captaincy of the Broadwater & Worthing Cricket Club from 1888, Mr A W F Somerset recalled: 'Then came the typhoid epidemic, and

the breaking up of the Broadwater & Worthing Club.'[5] Even the greatly anticipated Annual Rowing Regatta was a casualty:

> 'In the present depressed condition of affairs in the town a diminished interest in the annual regatta was inevitable. It must be many years since so small an attendance of spectators has been seen at this popular festival, very few visitors coming in from neighbouring towns to witness the sport provided. The beach was practically deserted, and only 1,073 persons paid for admission to the Pier, this being fewer by 2,645 than last year.'[6]

In chapter 2, Chris Hare – referring to the outcome of the November 1893 council elections – commented: 'The new council was quick to deliver.' One of their outstanding achievements was boldly commissioning the building, in 1896, of a new reservoir and pumping station at the foot of the Downs in Broadwater. That and a radical rehaul of the disposal of sewage meant Worthing could enjoy freedom from the curse of waterborne diseases such as typhoid. Meanwhile, the generosity of Edward Harrison who had made his land at Lyons Farm freely available to the council for the temporary provision of clean water was justly recognised on October 25th 1894 when he was given the accolade of being made the first Honorary Freeman of Worthing.[7]

As early as March 1894, with Dr Kelly reporting to Worthing Town Council Sanitary Committee that 'there was not a single case of typhoid (in Worthing)', the way was open to remove some ninety temporary water tanks that had been placed around the town.[8] The capacity of the tanks ranged from 150 to 200 gallons and, when they were put to auction,[9] they realised prices between 23 and 55 shillings. Then, in June, the *Worthing Gazette* printed a somewhat over-the-top, extended evocation of the merits of Worthing under the banner 'Worthing itself again' first aired in *Christian World*, but it did perhaps reflect an optimism for the future. Starting with:

> '"Well doctor how are things going now?" "Oh I haven't got half a day's work. The other doctors say just the same. They have to go golfing to fill up their time. I never knew the town so healthy as it is."'

It concluded with:

> 'Just now, Worthing is ruminating over the holding of a grand regatta during the Summer.'[10]

The annual regatta did go ahead, albeit delayed by one day to August 9th because of inclement weather, with: 'On the Pier and on the beach a considerable number of spectators congregated.'[11] Life was indeed gradually returning to normal but, in local books, there was a tendency to airbrush this episode out of the record at least for a generation. In 'Worthing Souvenir', designed to celebrate Queen Victoria's Diamond Jubilee, it was perhaps understandable that only a positive spin was put on 'Sanitary Progress' in Worthing and Dr Kelly's mortality figures were used selectively to paint a very positive picture about the 'Health of the Borough'.[12] Writing in 1938, however, the assistant medical officer of health had the confidence to say:

> 'The progressive increase in healthiness has not been interrupted in any noteworthy way, apart from a severe epidemic of typhoid fever, which ravaged the town in 1893.'[13]

Also in 1938, the *Worthing Gazette* invited a number of 'old residents' to reminisce about their earlier days in Worthing. Harry Hugh Parker Etherton – a retired, 80-year-old stone mason – was present when the 'Riot Act' was read on the steps of the Town

Hall in 1884 but I consider his thoughts about the typhoid epidemic are as good a way to conclude this book:

> 'The typhoid epidemic was in one way the making of Worthing in that it forced the Authorities of the time to put the water supply in order, a thing which might otherwise have not been done so speedily. It was, of course, a terrible time for the residents. It lasted for a considerable time and we felt the effects of it during the next few years. Visitors were few and far between, and hundreds of people left the town to find new homes. The opening of the new Waterworks at the foot of the Downs brought a sigh of relief and the town did not then take a very long time to remove the stigma which had been placed upon it. A few years later was the time when Worthing began to show the signs of becoming the fine town it is today.'[14]

1 See chapter 7.
2 Brighton Guardian & Hove Recorder for August 30th 1893
3 Worthing Herald for June 16th 1950
4 Worthing Gazette for December 23rd 1925
5 Worthing Gazette for June 6th 1934
6 Worthing Gazette for August 23rd 1893
7 Worthing Gazette for June 9th 1926
8 Worthing Gazette for March 7th 1894
9 Worthing Gazette for May 16th 1894
10 Worthing Gazette for June 27th 1894
11 Worthing Gazette for August 15th 1894
12 Worthing Souvenir published by Worthing Gazette in 1897
13 Eastwood, Cyril G in Worthing – a Survey of times past and present edited by Migeod, F W H 1938
14 Worthing Gazette for May 25th 1938

THE NEW SEWERAGE WORKS.

ARRIVAL OF THE DUKE AT THE RAILWAY STATION.

INSPECTION IN FRONT OF THE TOWN HALL.

THE FIRE BRIGADE DECORATION IN SOUTH STREET.

THE PUMPING STATION.

THE "VICTORIA" ENGINE

OPENING OF THE NEW WATERWORKS, APRIL 26TH, 1897 BY H.R.H. THE DUKE OF CAMBRIDGE, K.G.

Appendices
Broadwater and Worthing Cemetery

By Colin Reid

◀ *St Mary's Church, Broadwater (CR).*

▼ *Christ Church, Grafton Road (WL).*

During the nineteenth century, the population of Worthing had risen from 1,018 in 1801 to some 5,370 by 1851 and the principal burial ground for that period had been the churchyard surrounding St Mary's Church in Broadwater. From 1843, when Christ Church in Grafton Road opened, some additional but limited burial space became available. Meanwhile, at St Mary's Church, an Order in Council was given that, from April 1854, no further burials should be permitted except in vaults or brick graves where space allowed. As Rob Ferguson notes, this triggered two reactions: firstly, a piece of land

Rev Edward King Elliott, rector of St Mary's Church, Broadwater from 1853 to 1905, made lands available for the establishment of a burial ground in the parish (WSP).

Broadwater & Worthing Cemetery (1898), showing the original scope and extension of 1885. South Farm Road is adjacent to the left, while the road parallel on the right of this map is Broadwater Road (PR).

was purchased to the east of the churchyard from George Cortis and, secondly, consideration was given to the acquisition of land for the construction of a cemetery.[1]

Operating under the provisions of the Burials beyond the Metropolis Act [1852 with subsequent amendments], a Broadwater Parish Burial Board was established in 1861 and it had its first meeting in the vestry of St Mary's Church on May 23rd. On that occasion, William Tribe took the Chair and there was agreement that he and the following should be appointed to the board: George Heather, George Ede, Peter French, William Newland, George Burgess Bennett, Dr Henry James Collet, William High Bennett and Charles Ballard.

On May 28th, it was resolved that William Verrall be appointed clerk and registrar to the board. He was tasked to approach Thomas Wisden senior – owner of the Warren Farm Estate – to 'ascertain whether he is disposed to sell to this Board a piece of land being part of that estate for a burial ground for Broadwater Parish'. William Verrall was also asked to arrange that subsequent board meetings could use the Town Hall.

Initially, William Verrall and Peter French saw Thomas Wisden but he was indecisive and remained so after a further meeting when William Newland joined

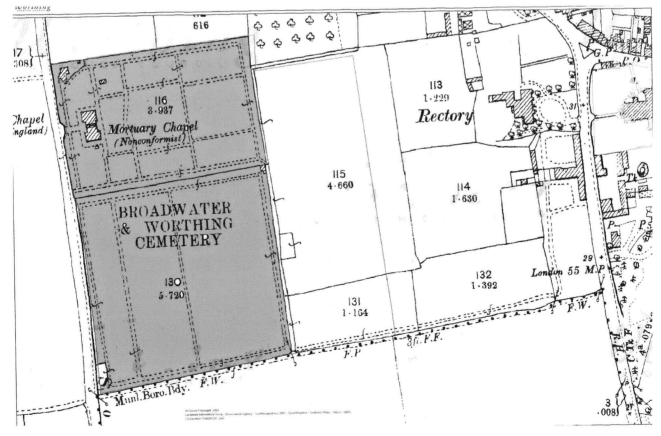

An early photograph of the cemetery chapels, with the Anglican chapel on the right and the Non-Conformist chapel on the left (PR).

them. As early as a meeting on June 10th, the board started looking elsewhere for land appropriate for a cemetery and, at their meeting on July 6th, it was resolved the Board should purchase the land offered by the Rev Edward King Elliott. This comprised four acres that abutted the eastern side of South Farm Road.

The board continued to meet regularly and operated diligently regarding issues such as: table of fees and charges, boundary walls, erection of chapels and a sexton's lodge, installation of iron gates, planting of plants, shrubs and trees, provision of paths and roads within the cemetery, appointment of a sexton and of gravediggers as necessary, inscriptions on and height of memorial stones etc.

The first sexton, James Stoner, took up his duties on May 11th 1863, and the first burials occurred on May 16th. After due deliberation, the board acquired land of more than five acres to extend the cemetery southward early in 1885. In March 1890,

◀ *In front of the lodge to Broadwater & Worthing Cemetery circa 1890, left to right are: James Stoner, Jane Sharpe, Caroline May Stoner, Caroline Virtue Stoner and John Stoner (sexton for the period of the typhoid epidemic) (WMA).*

John Stoner took over from his father as sexton. This then is how the cemetery was during the typhoid epidemic of 1893.

Following enactment of the Local Government Act 1894, the management of Broadwater and Worthing Cemetery came under the joint responsibility of the Borough of Worthing Town Council and Broadwater Parish Council. Accordingly, the new Burial Board met for the first time on March 29th 1895 and agreed that the new committee should consist of nine members – six appointed by the Town Council and three from the Parish Council. Initially, the Town Council members were: Alderman Piper and Councillors Fletcher (mayor), Butcher, Lyne, Smith and Walter, and the Parish representatives were: Richard Ballard, Henry George Apted and Michael King.

Then, under the terms of the Burial Act of 1900, responsibility for the cemetery transferred to Worthing Town Council on January 1st 1901, but there continued to be committee meetings jointly with members of the Parish Council until November 7th 1902. The Town Council oversaw the purchase of a further four acres to the east of the existing boundary in 1906, but it soon became evident that another site was needed. Durrington Cemetery on the Findon Road opened in 1927 and Worthing Crematorium was opened on the site of Muntham Court, Findon in 1967. Only a very tiny number of burials are now made at the Broadwater site where individuals had purchased grave space many years ago.

Friends of Broadwater & Worthing Cemetery

By Colin Reid

As the number of new burials at the Broadwater site declined during the twentieth century the cemetery became more and more overgrown such that the author found it something akin to an urban jungle in the mid-1990s. There were also incidents of vandalism culminating in the destruction of five Commonwealth War Gravestones. As Paul Holden and Tom Wye stated: 'The latter proved to be the catalyst that made so many people come forward and say "enough is enough"'.

October 24th 2008 was the inaugural meeting of the Friends of Broadwater and Worthing Cemetery under the chairmanship of retired Army Major Tom Wye MBE DL. From the earliest days, this has been a very active group. Prior to this book, the group has spawned three publications: *The A to Z of Broadwater and Worthing Cemetery, A History of Broadwater & Worthing Cemetery* and Broadwater and *Worthing Cemetery Military Burials & Inscriptions of the 20th Century World Wars*.

Each year from April through to October there have been very popular, Saturday, themed tours of the cemetery. Thus far, there have been some 60 such tours based on the work of a team of researchers who have contributed to the accompanying booklets. These tours have been supported by the sale of refreshments and literature. There have also been a number of guided tours on Sundays, some tours specifically relating to the flora and fauna and private tours for small groups and individuals.

FBWC is a member of the 'National Federation of Cemetery Friends', 'Worthing Heritage' and of 'Green Tides (Adur & Worthing Green Spaces

◀ *Cover for a typical tour Booklet – this one in 2011.*

Partnership)'. It has been very receptive to requests made by members of the public to locate the last resting place of relatives. Some members have given talks about the cemetery to local groups. Once a month teams of members and other volunteers have cleared swathes of vegetation to reveal long lost tombstones or in preparation for tours.

From the inception of the group, John Vaughan had produced *The Broadsheet* – the triannual voice of FBWC. Issue 44 published in the autumn of 2021 was the last such and is being replaced by a biannual newsletter. The chairmanship of the group transferred to Debra Hillman on October 19th 2012. She has fully supported the production and financing of this book and she was pleased to pen the Foreword.

Activity of FBWC in Pictures

▲ *Horse-drawn hearse supplied by Ian Hart Funeral Directors for the cemetery's 150th Anniversary Tour. [May 11th 2013] JH).*

◀◀ *Lottery-funded pioneers of FBWC. L to R: Tom Wye, Mary Mckeown, Pam Stepney, John Vaughan, Sue Nea, Judith Skitt, Rosemary Westlake, Denise McGrath, John Stepney, Debra Hillman, Sue Baker, Phil Skitt, Sally Roberts, Rosemary Pearson, Angela Butler, Angela Shaw, Frank Ffitch. [March 13th 2010] (KM).*

◀ *Loyal toast to Her Majesty Queen Elizabeth II by John Vaughan, celebrating 60 glorious years as our Queen. [June 2nd 2012] (JV).*

▲ Worthing Corps Salvation Army Band – tree planting in memory of Capt Sarah Jane Broadhurst who died in 1892 following a severe assault in Shoreham at the hands of Worthing's Skeleton Army. [May 11th 2013] (JH).

▲ Everyday attire for Paul Robards, Sally Roberts, Rosemary Westlake, John Vaughan and Mary Mckeown. [May 11th 2013] (JH).

▲ Representatives of Co-op Funeral Care that paid for the supply and installation of a memorial stone to those who perished in the 1893 typhoid epidemic. [July 6th 2013] (DH).

▲ Display board for the cemetery tour commemorating the 120th Anniversary of the 1893 typhoid epidemic. [July 6th 2013] (JV).

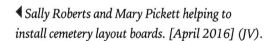

◀ Sally Roberts and Mary Pickett helping to install cemetery layout boards. [April 2016] (JV).

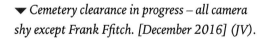

▼ Cemetery clearance in progress – all camera shy except Frank Ffitch. [December 2016] (JV).

◀ Any excuse to dress up – a Sunday tour of the cemetery – Debra Hillman, Mary Mckeown, Sally Roberts and Rosemary Pearson. [2017] (JH).

▲◥ Uncanny resemblance – Colin Reid impersonating his Gt, Gt Grandfather Edward Payne (1844 to 1922) for the 'Relatively Speaking' Cemetery Tour. [July 1st 2017] (CR).

▶ Queens of refreshments – Karen Foster and Carole Manning. [September 2nd 2017] (JV).

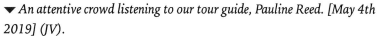

▲ Who said clearance was hard work? Posing for the camera: Paul Robards, unknown, unknown, Barbara Shaw, unknown, Frank Ffitch, Karen Foster and Joss Lambourne. [March 2019] (JV).

▼ An attentive crowd listening to our tour guide, Pauline Reed. [May 4th 2019] (JV).

▲ Here Frank Ffitch & Gill Heasman are about to place artificial markers at unmarked graves for a tour. [April 7th 2018] (GH).

▲ A Service of Remembrance by the memorial cross. [November 2019] (JV).

▼ Selling tour booklets (62 & counting) – Anne Powell and Rosemary Pearson. [August 3rd 2019] (JV).

▲ *Debra & Jeff Hillman delivering typhoid grave markers. [September 2nd 2022] (MM).*

◀ *Grave markers produced by Debra Hillman for the 164 typhoid victims buried in the cemetery. [September 2nd 2022] (MM).*

▲ *Jeff Hillman, Paul Robards and Colin Reid hammering stakes into hard ground to receive the markers. [September 2nd 2022] (GH).*

▲ *Of the 164 typhoid victims buried in the Cemetery, 98 were laid to rest in section A7. Here are some of those. [September 3rd 2022] (MM).*

▲ *Isabella Coppard 'Peacefully fell asleep, safe in the arms of Jesus, Sunday Evening October 22nd'. One of the stories told on the cemetery tour. [September 3rd 2022] (MM).*

◀ *On the 2022 typhoid tour, Colin is being videoed at one of the featured grave sites. [September 3rd 2022] (SR).*

Select Bibliography

Davies, Roger, *Tarring – a Walk through its History* (Roger W Davies 1990)

Elleray, D Robert, *A Millennium Encyclopaedia of Worthing History* (Optimus Books 1998)

Ferguson, Rob, *Placed for a Purpose – the History of Broadwater Church and its Parish* (Teamwork Craftbooks 2018)

Fox-Wilson, Frank, *The Story of Goring and Highdown* (Goring Book Association 1987)

Hare, Chris, *Worthing, A History* (Phillimore 2008)

Hare, Chris, *Worthing in the Bad Old Days - Riot, Beer and the Word of God* (Christ Church Parochial Outreach Committee 2021)

Holden, Paul, *Typhoid, Bombs and Matron – the History of Worthing Hospital* (1992)

Huxley-Williams, Muriel G, *A Brief Story of Heene in the County of Sussex* (Rodney Press 1973)

Keech, Barrie, *Doctors, Dentists and Death – West Sussex Health Issues since the 19th Century* (West Sussex County Council 2011)

Kelly, Charles M D, F R C P, *Report on the Epidemic of Enteric Fever in 1893 in the Borough of Worthing in Broadwater and West Tarring* (The Southern Publishing Company 1894)

Kerridge, Ronald and Standing, Michael, *Worthing from Saxon Settlement to Seaside Town* (Optimus Books 2000)

Migeod, F W H, *Worthing – a Survey of Times Past and Present* (The Southern Publishing Company 1938)

Taylor, Rupert, *Centenary – One Hundred Years of the Borough of Worthing* (Beckett Features, T R Beckett Ltd 1990)

Thomson, Theodore Dr, *Report to the Local Government Board on an Epidemic of Enteric Fever in the Borough of Worthing and in the Villages of Broadwater and West Tarring* (OHMS 1894)

White, Sally, *Worthing Past* (Phillimore 2000)

Woolgar, Marion, *Afflicted Worthing in Thomas Evans and his Epidemic Relief Fund 1893/94 for West Sussex Archives Society Journal No 79* (2011)

Index

A

absent 28, 29, 107, 111
leave of absence 29, 59, 111, 113, 117
acquisition (property) 34, 124, 125
Ade, Eleanor
Afflicted Worthing 12, 80
agriculture 67, 98
agricultural labourer 40, 51
Alabaster, Henry 105
alderman 16, 17, 33, 35-37, 45-47, 57, 73-76, 116, 126
Allen, Lilian 98
All Saints Church 47, 50, 51
Altrincham 80, 81
ambulance 2, 44, 45
Anderson, Edith 28, 29, 32, 33
Angmering 96
Ann Street 33, 59, 71
antibiotics 19, 106
anxiety 17, 46, 52, 78
apprentice 55, 80, 97, 100
Arundel 36, 75, 96, 97
asylum 53, 107
auction 30, 47, 62, 119

authorities 10, 13, 28, 35, 95, 113, 118, 120

B

bacteria 19, 27, 95, 98
bacterial infection 18, 46
bacterium 18, 19
Baker, James 35-37
bakers (profession) 100, 105, 110
baptism 47-50, 53
Bartletts 98
Bath Place 71, 107
Beach, Harry and Kate 105
beach (see: sea - seashore)
bedding 39, 62
Bedford Row 41, 43
beef tea 66, 71, 74, 75, 78, 108
Birmingham 48, 81
Bishop, Helena 98
blacksmith 54
boatmen 74, 78, 118
boiling 29, 66, 108
Bonfire societies/clubs 32, 37, 76, 77, 113
bookseller 47, 80

Bournemouth 76, 83
Bowel/intestinal perforation 19, 95
Braby, Ernest 108
brandy 75, 76, 78
Brazier, Edith 29, 111
Brazier, Florence 30
bread 35, 78, 110
Breads, Owen 24, 25, 35, 37
bricklayer 100, 102
brickmaker 90, 100
brick-setters 26
Bridlington 80-82
Brighton 18, 40, 47, 75-77, 79, 112, 113, 117, 118
Broadbridge, Ellen 30, 39, 104
Broadbridge, George 39, 40
Broadwater 10, 17, 18, 27, 28, 31, 34, 43, 47, 50, 56, 57, 66, 68, 69, 79, 85, 87-89, 93, 94, 96-98, 101, 104, 105, 108, 110, 117-119, 123, 124, 126
Broadwater & Worthing Cemetery 9, 12, 47, 48, 58, 94, 104, 105, 123-127
Broadwater Cemetery 13, 21, 39, 47, 58, 107